America's National Parks

HAWAI`I VOLCANOES
NATIONAL PARK

Adventure, Explore, Discover

STEPHEN FEINSTEIN

MyReportLinks.com Books
an imprint of

  Enslow Publishers, Inc.
Box 398, 40 Industrial Road
Berkeley Heights, NJ 07922
USA

MyReportLinks.com Books, an imprint of Enslow Publishers, Inc. MyReportLinks®
is a registered trademark of Enslow Publishers, Inc.

Library of Congress Cataloging-in-Publication Data

Feinstein, Stephen.
  Hawaii Volcanoes National Park / Stephen Feinstein.
      p. cm. — (America's national parks : adventure, explore, discover)
  Summary: "A virtual tour of Hawaii Volcanoes National Park, with chapters devoted to the
history of this region, history of the park, plant and animal life, environmental problems facing the
park, and activities in the area"—Provided by publisher.
  Includes bibliographical references and index.
  ISBN-13: 978-1-59845-094-1 (hardcover)
  ISBN-10: 1-59845-094-8 (hardcover)
  1. Hawaii Volcanoes National Park (Hawaii)—Juvenile literature. I. Title.
  DU628.H33F45 2008
  919.69'1—dc22
                                    2007038836

Printed in the United States of America

10 9 8 7 6 5 4 3 2 1

To Our Readers:
Through the purchase of this book, you and your library gain access to the Report Links that specifically back up
this book.
The Publisher will provide access to the Report Links that back up this book and will keep these Report Links up
to date on **www.myreportlinks.com** for five years from the book's first publication date.
We have done our best to make sure all Internet addresses in this book were active and appropriate when
we went to press. However, the author and the Publisher have no control over, and assume no liability for, the
material available on those Internet sites or on other Web sites they may link to.
The usage of the MyReportLinks.com Books Web site is subject to the terms and conditions stated on the Usage
Policy Statement on **www.myreportlinks.com**.
A password may be required to access the Report Links that back up this book. The password is found on the
bottom of page 4 of this book.
Any comments or suggestions can be sent by e-mail to comments@myreportlinks.com or to the address on the
back cover.

♻ Enslow Publishers, Inc., is committed to printing our books on recycled paper. The paper in every book
contains 10% to 30% post-consumer waste (PCW). The cover board on the outside of each book contains 100%
PCW. Our goal is to do our part to help young people and the environment too!

Photo Credits: © Corel Corporation, pp. 1, 6–7, 8–9, 13, 16–17, 20–21, 42–43, 86, 96–97, 108–109;
Enslow Publishers, Inc., p. 5 (inset); Hawaiian Ecosystems at Risk (HEAR) Project, p. 92; Hawaii Audubon
Society, p. 79; Hawaii Center for Volcanology, p. 60; Hawaii Visitors and Convention Bureau, p. 105;
Library of Congress, pp. 46–47, 50; MyReportLinks.com Books, p. 4; National Park
Foundation, p. 88; National Parks Conservation Association, p. 90; National Park Service, pp. 5, 53, 55,
95, 99; NOAA, p. 102; Photos.com, pp. 3, 6a, 7a, 24–25, 30–31, 37, 62–63, 112–113; Project Gutenberg
Literary Archive Foundation, p. 36; Shutterstock.com, pp. 6b, 6c, 7b, 7c, 34–35, 66, 72–73, 76, 80–81,
84, 100–101, and chapter opening photos of electronics; Smithsonian National Museum of Natural
History, p. 70; Surf News Network, p. 114; The Hawaiian Historical Society, p. 39; The Mariners' Museum,
p. 45; The Nature Conservancy, p. 93; The New York Times Company, p. 58; University of Hawai'i at
Manoa, p. 68; University of Texas Libraries, p. 57; USA.gov, p. 48; U.S. Department of the Interior/U.S.
Geological Survey, pp. 11, 15, 27, 32, 74, 83; Volcano Gallery, p. 22; World Triathlon Corporation, p. 116.

Cover Photo: © Corel Corporation

CONTENTS

MyReportLinks.com Books
Great Books, Great Links, Great for Research!

The Internet sites featured in this book can save you hours of research time. These Internet sites—we call them **"Report Links"**—are constantly changing, but we keep them up to date on our Web site.

When you see this "Approved Web Site" logo, you will know that we are directing you to a great Internet site that will help you with your research.

Give it a try! Type http://www.myreportlinks.com into your browser, click on the series title and enter the password, then click on the book title, and scroll down to the Report Links listed for this book.

The Report Links will bring you to great source documents, photographs, and illustrations. MyReportLinks.com Books save you time, feature Report Links that are kept up to date, and make report writing easier than ever! A complete listing of the Report Links can be found on pages 118–119 at the back of the book.

Please see "To Our Readers" on the copyright page for important information about this book, the MyReportLinks.com Web site, and the Report Links that back up this book.

Please enter **HVP1825** if asked for a password.

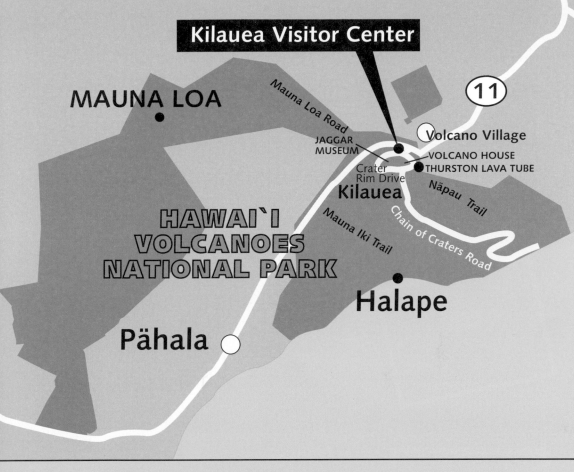

Kilauea Visitor Center

MAUNA LOA

Mauna Loa Road

(11)

Volcano Village

JAGGAR
MUSEUM

VOLCANO HOUSE
THURSTON LAVA TUBE

Crater
Rim Drive

Kilauea

Nāpau Trail

HAWAI`I
VOLCANOES
NATIONAL PARK

Mauna Iki Trail

Chain of Craters Road

Halape

Pähala

Kauai
◆ Mount
Waialeale

Niihau

Oahu
Honolulu ★ ◆ Diamond
Head   Molokai

North
↑

Lanai City ●
Lanai

● Kahului
Maui

Kahoolawe

PACIFIC OCEAN

◆ Mauna Kea
● Hilo
Hawaii
Mauna Loa ◆
● Kilauea

HAWAI`I
VOLCANOES
NATIONAL PARK

Key
◆ = Volcano

The top map shows the main points of interest at Hawai`i Volcanoes
National Park. The inset provides the location of the park in relation
to the rest of the Hawaiian Islands.

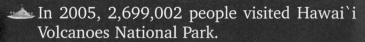

- Hawai`i Volcanoes National Park is located on the island of Hawai`i, in the state of Hawaii.

- The park was established on August 1, 1916.

- The area set aside for the park covers 330,000 acres (133,000 hectares); 505 square miles (1,348 square kilometers).

- In 2005, 2,699,002 people visited Hawai`i Volcanoes National Park.

- There are two active volcanoes at the park. Kilauea reaches a peak of 4,190 feet (1,277 meters). It has been erupted since January 3, 1983. The second volcano is Mauna Loa, with a peak of 13,677 feet (3,962 meters). Mauna Loa most recently erupted in March 1984.

- Two kinds of lava can be found in the parks volcanoes: a'a and pahoehoe.

- The most common species of plant life found in the park are the hapuu tree fern, ohia lehua tree, koa tree, mamane tree, mamake (nettle), pukiawe shrub, akala (raspberry), and the ohelo berry.

- Popular animals species abundant in the park include:

    Birds: apapane, amakihi, nene (Hawaiian goose, state bird), elepaio, iiwi, io (Hawaiian hawk), uau (Hawaiian dark-rumped petrel), white-tailed tropic bird

    Mammals: opeapea (Hawaiian hoary bat), ilio holu i ka uaua (Hawaiian monk seal), Humpback whale (November–May)

Turtles: honuea (hawksbill turtle), honu (green sea turtle)

Spider: happy-face spider

The climate is generally warm and moist, although the temperature varies with elevation. For example, the temperatures are tropical at sea level, and cool as the elevation increases. Winter snow can be found on the summit of Mauna Loa. The windward side of the island of Hawai`i is among the rainiest parts of the United States. The leeward side of the island is very dry.

There are two main roads on which to take scenic drives of Hawai`i Volcanoes National Park: Crater Rim Drive and Chain of Craters Road.

Many hiking trails wind their way through the park. The most popular are Keauhou Trail, Kilauea Iki Trail, Mauna Iki Trail, Mauna Loa Trail, and Napau Trail.

Chapter

1

Travelers come from all over the world in hopes of witnessing an eruption of Kilauea like this one.

The World's Most Active Volcano

Throughout the years, travelers with an interest in volcanoes have been coming to the island of Hawai`i from all over the world. Many are there to witness an eruption of Kilauea. One such visitor was the famous writer Mark Twain. From his vantage point on the rim of Kilauea's caldera, or volcanic crater, he marveled at the amazing spectacle below. Hot lava was bursting forth from the lava lake that filled the bottom of Halemaumau crater.

Awed by the power of the volcanic eruption, Twain described what he saw:

> Stretching away before us, was a heaving sea of molten fire of seemingly limitless extent . . . now and then the surging bosom of the lake under our noses would calm down ominously and seem to be gathering strength for an enterprise; and then all of a sudden a red dome of lava of the bulk of an ordinary dwelling would heave

itself aloft like an escaping balloon, then burst asunder . . . the crashing plunge of the ruined dome into the lake again would send a world of seething billows lashing against the shores and shaking the foundations of our perch.[1]

Kilauea is one of two active volcanoes located in Hawai`i Volcanoes National Park, on the southeast side of the island of Hawai`i. Within the park's 330,000 acres (133,000 hectares) is another active volcano, Mauna Loa. Kilauea's summit is 4,190 feet (1,277 meters) above sea level. It is the world's most active volcano, with a long history of frequent eruptions. *Kilauea* means "much spreading" or "spewing" in Hawaiian, referring to the volcanic eruptions.

Like the other Hawaiian volcanoes, Kilauea is known as a shield volcano. It appears to resemble a warrior's shield lying on the ground. Eruptions of shield volcanoes are relatively quiet compared to the explosive, fiery eruptions of steep, cone-shaped volcanoes, such as Mount Pinatubo in the Philippines or Mount Saint Helens in the state of Washington.

During a shield volcano eruption, red-hot lava fountains and flows out of cracks in the earth's crust. As time goes by, the cooled lava from numerous eruptions gradually builds the shield volcano into a huge mountain that is much wider than it is tall. Eruptions of Kilauea are usually not

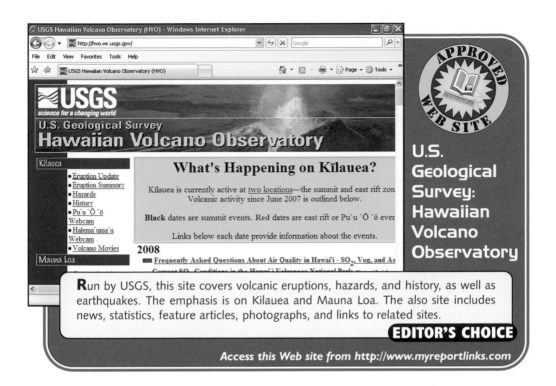

USGS Hawaiian Volcano Observatory (HVO) - Windows Internet Explorer

http://hvo.wr.usgs.gov/

File Edit View Favorites Tools Help

USGS Hawaiian Volcano Observatory (HVO)

USGS
science for a changing world
U.S. Geological Survey
Hawaiian Volcano Observatory

Kilauea
• Eruption Update
• Eruption Summary
• Hazards
• History
• Pu'u 'Ō 'ō
  Webcam
• Halema'uma'u
  Webcam
• Volcano Movies

Mauna Loa

What's Happening on Kīlauea?

Kilauea is currently active at two locations—the summit and east rift zon
Volcanic activity since June 2007 is outlined below.

Black dates are summit events. **Red dates** are east rift or Pu'u 'Ō 'ō ever

Links below each date provide information about the events.

2008
Frequently Asked Questions About Air Quality in Hawai'i - SO₂, Vog, and As

U.S. Geological Survey: Hawaiian Volcano Observatory

Run by USGS, this site covers volcanic eruptions, hazards, and history, as well as earthquakes. The emphasis is on Kilauea and Mauna Loa. The also site includes news, statistics, feature articles, photographs, and links to related sites.

EDITOR'S CHOICE

Access this Web site from http://www.myreportlinks.com

very explosive. It is often possible to approach near enough to get a close-up view of the volcanic activity.

Twain was also impressed with the wild beauty of Kilauea's eruption. His vivid description captured details of the radiant colors of the lava oozing down the sides of the volcano:

> Here and there were gleaming holes twenty feet in diameter, broken in the dark crust, and in them the melted lava—the color a dazzling white just tinged with yellow—was boiling and surging furiously; and from these holes branched numberless bright torrents in many directions . . . we could see that they ran down small, steep hills and were genuine cataracts of fire, white at their source, but soon

cooling and turning to the richest red, grained with alternate lines of black and gold.[2]

Although most of Kilauea's eruptions have not been violent, there have been some exceptions. Thomas Augustus Jaggar, who in 1912 became one of the first scientists to study Hawaii's volcanoes, wrote that "even Kilauea is not guiltless of terrific and destructive explosive eruption. Around 1790 thousands of tons of gravel and boulders and dust were strewn over Hawaii from Kilauea, covering hundreds of square miles, destroying the vegetation, and killing some of the people."[3] This violent eruption formed a lava lake in Kilauea's summit caldera, the lake that was later observed by Mark Twain.

In 1868 an eruption at Kilauea accompanied a strong earthquake. It was an unusual eruption in that it consisted of mud instead of lava. People called it "the great mudflow." In the words of an observer at the time: "In the midst of the great earthquake we saw burst out of the top of [a precipice] . . . an immense river of . . . red earth . . . , which rushed down in headlong course and across the plain below, . . . swallowing up everything in its way—trees, houses, cattle, horses, men, in an instant as it were. It went three miles in not more than three minutes' time."[4]

Kilauea's molten lava lake at Halemaumau lasted until 1924, when another violent, explosive

The Star of the Sea "Painted" Church was once part of the Village of Kalapana. As the lava flow advanced in 1990 the church was moved to Kaimu, Hawaii, so that it would not be destroyed.

eruption occurred. An enormous, turbulent column of ash, steam, and rocks erupted from the summit when water invaded the magma chamber below the summit. The eruption drained the lava lake.

THE LONGEST VOLCANIC ERUPTION

On January 3, 1983, the Kilauea volcano began its most recent eruption. The eruption was known as the Puu Oo eruption. It began from a fissure of that name on the volcano's southeast flank in Kilauea's east rift zone. Except for occasional short pauses, the eruption has continued to this day. This makes it the longest volcanic rift eruption in recorded history. Lava from the eruption has added more than 600 acres (243 hectares) of lava and black sand beach to the island's southeastern shore. The lava has buried 43 square miles (111 square kilometers) of land, including 16,000 acres (6,475 hectares) of lowland and rain forest. The lava has destroyed more than two hundred homes, including the entire Village of Kalapana in 1990.

MAUNA LOA

The island of Hawaii's other active volcano, Mauna Loa, is the world's most massive volcano, and the world's biggest mountain. It is 60 miles (97 kilometers) long and 30 miles (48 kilometers) wide. Hawaiians long ago gave Mauna Loa its

Mauna Loa Volcano, Hawai`i - Windows Internet Explorer

http://hvo.wr.usgs.gov/maunaloa/

File   Edit   View   Favorites   Tools   Help

Mauna Loa Volcano, Hawai`i

Page ▾   Tools ▾

USGS
science for a changing world
Hawaiian Volcano Observatory

Mauna Loa

Mauna Loa
Earth's Largest Volcano

Kilauea

Mauna Loa
• Current
  Activity
• Hazards
• History
• Summit
  Panorama

Earthquakes

Other
Volcano

Mauna Loa is important because it is the biggest volcano. **The Mauna Loa: USGS Hawaiian Volcano Observatory** Web page covers volcanic activity, hazards, and history. There is also a live panoramic view of the summit of the volcano.

name, which means "Long Mountain" in Hawaiian, most likely because of its long, gently sloping shape. From its base at the bottom of the ocean, Mauna Loa rises 56,000 feet (17,069 meters) to its summit, about .75 miles (1.2 kilometers) taller than Mount Everest. At 13,677 feet (3,962 meters) above sea level, Mauna Loa's summit has a subarctic climate. Snow can fall any time of year.

The most recent eruption of Mauna Loa occurred in March 1984 after a quiet period that lasted nine years. The eruption began at night

Hardened Pahoehoe Lava at Hawai`i Volcanoes National Park. Park rangers often carve trails through the hardened lava for visitors to walk on.

with a line of lava fountains at the summit, 50 to 70 feet (15 to 21 meters) high. The lava fountains created a curtain of fire, lighting up the night sky with a fiery glow. Lava flows extended many miles down the mountain, threatening the city of Hilo. Fortunately, the eruption stopped before the lava reached the outskirts of town.

➡ Hiking to the Lava Flow

Visitors to Hawai`i Volcanoes National Park enjoy an incredible variety of sights. Besides the two active volcanoes, within the park are black-sand beaches, a rugged coastline, and spectacular cliffs known as *pali*. There are luxuriant rain forests with exotic tropical vegetation. And there are dozens of craters and cinder cones, hills piled high with pumice, a desert, and vast areas of hardened lava. After experiencing these and many other fascinating sights, adventurous visitors might have an opportunity to hike out across the hardened lava to see molten lava flowing into the sea.

Sometimes, park rangers mark a trail across the hardened lava to an observation point. From there you might see the flowing lava. The rangers will advise you about current volcanic activity and what to watch out for. The trail begins at the end of the Chain of Craters Road. This road leads from the summit of Kilauea down toward the ocean. The road descends 3,700 feet (1,128 meters) as it winds through fern forests and past many small craters. It ends at a hardened lava flow near the coast. The road used to go as far as Kalapana on the coast. But starting in 1986, lava flows buried the road beyond this point. The flows cover 8.7 miles (14 kilometers) of highway with lava as dccp as 115 feet (35 meters).

At the end of the road there is a barricade and an information booth. In the distance you might see steam rising high above the waves as hot lava splashes into the sea. The park rangers prefer that you not venture across the hardened lava. But they will permit you to do so depending on the level of volcanic activity. Some days are safer than others because conditions are always changing. Since volcanic activity is unpredictable, this hike can be dangerous unless you are prepared for local conditions.

The hike to the lava flow can be long and hard. Getting there and back can take several hours. During the day it can be very hot. There is no shade along the way, and the black lava reflects the sun's heat. You should bring enough water, at least 2 quarts (about 1.89 liters), to avoid dehydration. The rangers advise wearing long pants and a hat, and suggest that you bring along a first-aid kit.

At night, you must carry a flashlight and several extra batteries. The lava underfoot will tear at

The Kalapana coast is now one of
Hawaii's black-sand beaches.

Aloha Volcano Gallery and Hawaii Visitor Information, Volcano Village, Big Island of Hawaii - Windows Internet E...

http://www.volcanogallery.com/

File   Edit   View   Favorites   Tools   Help

Aloha Volcano Gallery and Hawaii Visitor Information, ...

Page ▾ Tools ▾

Aloha! Volcano Gallery - Volcano, Hawaii

The "local" source for Kilauea Volcano Hawaii Visitor Information and Hawaiian Gifts Directory **

Volcano Gallery, P.O. Box 699, Volcano Village, Big Island of Hawaii 96785 - (808) 967-8617

Read / Sign our Guest Book   Search our site   FREE Newsletter   Email Us

Volcano Weather Update

Hawaii Volcanoes National Park

Hawaii Volcanoes National Park Directory and Visitor Information

Volcano Vacation Houses / B&B's

Volcano Lodging Directory (A complete list of "Quality Approved" "Choice" Vacation Houses and Bed and Breakfast (B&Bs) in the Volcano area). Rooms from $65 / night! - Cottages from $95 / night! - Houses from $110 / night!

Handcrafted Hawaiian

Shop at Volcano Gall

"Gia

Billed as the "local" source for Kilauea Volcano and Hawaii visitor information, **Aloha! Volcano Gallery** covers the island and park, volcano tours and conditions, and Volcano Village. It provides video clips, live cameras, and links to related sites.

the bottom of your shoes. You will have to watch your footing carefully to avoid spraining an ankle or falling. There are sharp jags and cracks and holes in the brittle surface of the lava. You will hike across a type of lava called pahoehoe, which can mold itself into fantastic shapes. It consists of smooth, glassy, ropelike coils and swirls. Pahoehoe lava is the type of lava that most often flows from lava lakes.

As you hike across the hardened lava, do not walk too close to the edge above the sea. The lava crust forms unstable ledges known as lava benches. These can collapse into the ocean without warning. When you reach the observation point, do not go any farther. The closer you go to the lava flow, the more dangerous it gets. When the molten lava with a temperature of 2,100°F (1,149°C) hits the surface of the ocean, there is an explosive reaction. Scalding water shoots up hundreds of feet. Chunks of lava are also hurled high into the air. Also, when lava reaches the sea, the resulting mix of hydrochloric acid with the air can be toxic.

Over the years, a number of hikers have been injured, some even killed, while hiking to the lava flow. But if you are careful, you will be rewarded by the dramatic sight of the lava flowing into the sea. At night, the glowing red lava is especially spectacular.

Chapter

2

An eruption of Mt. Kilauea is a jaw-dropping sight.

History of the Hawaiian Islands

Most visitors are drawn to Hawaii by the islands' beauty and serenity. Vacationers go to Hawaii expecting the islands to be a tropical paradise, the perfect place for relaxation and fun. Writer John Calderazzo first went to Hawaii to study the volcanoes on the island of Hawai`i. He immediately fell in love with Hawaii, the typical reaction of most first-time visitors:

[T]his was our first time in Hawaii. But the second I stepped off the plane at Hilo, on the Big Island, I wished I had been coming my entire life. Tremendous bursts of pink and orange bougainvillea spilled over walls of volcanic rock. Slender palms swayed in ocean breezes. Blood-red anthurium flowers and shiny green elephant ears dominated every garden.[1]

Mark Twain, too, was enchanted with the beauty of the Hawaiian Islands. He called them "the loveliest fleet of islands that lies anchored in any ocean."[2] But these peaceful islands were created by the most violent and powerful forces in nature. And those forces are still active, mainly on the island of Hawai`i.

GEOLOGIC HISTORY: THE HOT SPOT

During the 1960s, scientists developed the theory of plate tectonics. This is the idea that the earth's crust is made up of interlocking tectonic plates that are slowly moving. There are seven gigantic plates and numerous smaller ones. These plates are large slabs of solid rock that float on and travel over the mantle. The mantle is the layer of the earth that lies between the crust and the core. The continents and ocean floors, part of the crust, are embedded in the constantly moving plates.

The Hawaiian Islands are actually the tips of huge mountains created by molten rock spewing out of the mantle. The islands began rising from the ocean more than 70 million years ago. In 1963 J. Tuzo Wilson, a Canadian geophysicist, had a theory. He proposed that the Hawaiian Islands were formed when the Pacific Plate moved slowly west-northwestward over a hot spot.[3] Scientists today know of at least one hundred hot spots under various parts of the earth's crust. One of

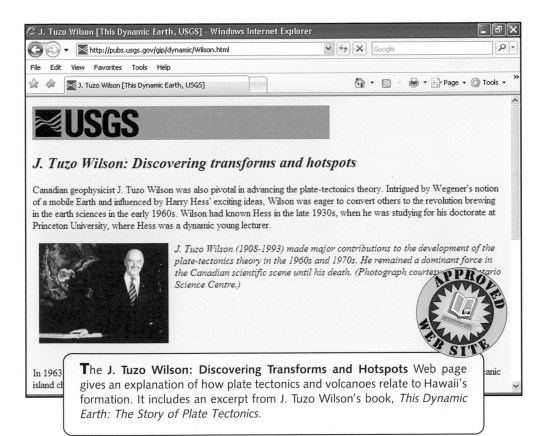

≋USGS

J. Tuzo Wilson: Discovering transforms and hotspots

Canadian geophysicist J. Tuzo Wilson was also pivotal in advancing the plate-tectonics theory. Intrigued by Wegener's notion of a mobile Earth and influenced by Harry Hess' exciting ideas, Wilson was eager to convert others to the revolution brewing in the earth sciences in the early 1960s. Wilson had known Hess in the late 1930s, when he was studying for his doctorate at Princeton University, where Hess was a dynamic young lecturer.

J. Tuzo Wilson (1908-1993) made major contributions to the development of the plate-tectonics theory in the 1960s and 1970s. He remained a dominant force in the Canadian scientific scene until his death. (Photograph courtesy ...tario Science Centre.)

In 1963 ... island cl...

The **J. Tuzo Wilson: Discovering Transforms and Hotspots** Web page gives an explanation of how plate tectonics and volcanoes relate to Hawaii's formation. It includes an excerpt from J. Tuzo Wilson's book, *This Dynamic Earth: The Story of Plate Tectonics.*

them lies below the Hawaiian Islands, currently beneath Hawai`i Island. And Kilauea is directly over the hot spot.

As the Pacific Plate passes over the hot spot, molten rock bursts through weak spots in the crust, forming volcanoes. The hot spot is actually a column of solid rock that rises slowly upward from possibly as deep as 2,200 miles (3,541 kilo-meters) below the earth's surface, at the boundary between the core and the mantle. The rock column moves upward through the mantle because it is hotter than the surrounding mantle. The rock stays solid and cannot melt because of the tremendous pressures.

Near the top, about 60 miles (97 kilometers) below the surface, the pressures are low enough so that the rock melts. The hot, melted rock, or magma, eventually rises to the surface. There the magma erupts in the form of lava flows or fountains. The hot-spot column is stationary in relation to the earth's core. As the plate slowly moves above the hot spot, the column of magma leaves a trace on the crust. This trace has taken the form of a string of islands—a volcanic island chain.

THE PACIFIC PLATE

The Pacific Plate is moving northwest at about 3.5 inches (9 centimeters) a year. Once the Pacific Plate carries an island far enough away from the hot spot, volcanic activity on the island subsides and eventually stops. Volcanoes on the oldest Hawaiian Islands, those farthest away from the hot spot, are extinct. Haleakala, the volcano on Maui, the island closest to the island of Hawai`i and created just before, is dormant. It may erupt again. But Haleakala is in the process of becoming extinct as Maui moves farther away from the hot spot.

The island of Hawai`i is the youngest of the Hawaiian Islands. It was formed by five volcanoes:

Kohala, Hualalai, Mauna Kea, Mauna Loa, and Kilauea. Kohala and Mauna Kea are extinct. Hualalai, which last erupted in 1801, is dormant. Kilauea and Mauna Loa, of course, are very active. The island's volcanoes began growing over the hot spot about a half million years ago. Sometime in the prehistoric past, Kilauea's summit collapsed, leaving a caldera 2 miles (3 kilometers) wide and 2.5 miles (4 kilometers) long. Within this caldera is Halemaumau, a pit within a crater. As the island drifts with the Pacific Plate over the hot spot, it will eventually become disconnected to the earth's rising heat. This may happen a hundred thousand years or perhaps a million years in the future.

⊜ A NEW MOUNTAIN

The hot spot has a diameter of about 50 miles (80 kilometers). A new island on the periphery of the hot spot is being born less than 30 miles (48 kilometers) southeast of the island of Hawaii. A volcano named Loihi has already risen 15,000 feet (4,572 meters) above the ocean floor. Loihi is a seamount, a mountain on the floor of the ocean that does not yet reach above the surface. Within ten thousand years, at its current rate of growth, Loihi will break the surface of the ocean. And there will be a brand new addition to the Hawaiian Islands.

Haleakala is a well-known volcano on Hawaii's island of Maui. Unlike Kilauea, Haleakala is a dormant volcano soon to become extinct.

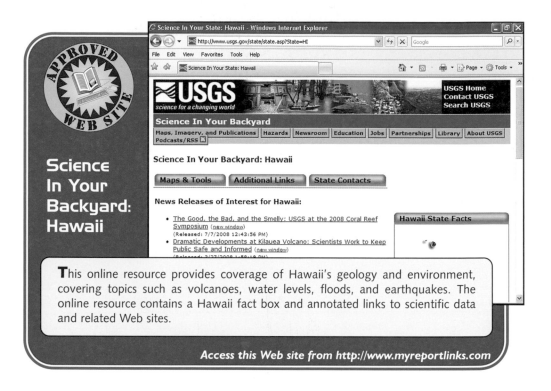

Science
In Your
Backyard:
Hawaii

This online resource provides coverage of Hawaii's geology and environment, covering topics such as volcanoes, water levels, floods, and earthquakes. The online resource contains a Hawaii fact box and annotated links to scientific data and related Web sites.

Access this Web site from http://www.myreportlinks.com

➔THE FIRST HAWAIIANS

Hawaii's first human inhabitants arrived at the islands about 1,600 years ago. They were Polynesians from the Marquesas Islands in the middle of the Pacific Ocean. The Polynesians had sailed 3,000 miles (4,828 kilometers) to the Hawaiian Islands in huge double-hulled canoes. According to ancient legend, the name of the islands comes from Hawaii Loa. He was the navigator who led the first Polynesian expedition. These first Hawaiians were then joined about a thousand years later by Polynesians from Tahiti.

When the Polynesians arrived in Hawaii, they found a primitive, untouched land. There were deep canyons, lofty mountains, fertile valleys, and abundant forests. The valleys provided rich and productive lands for agriculture. The surrounding waters provided an abundance of food. In the higher regions of the mountains, the Polynesians obtained logs for their canoes and stone for their tools. And in the caldera of Kilauea, they found the fire pit called Halemaumau, the abode of their goddess Pele.

THE LAND OF PELE

The ancient Hawaiians knew nothing about the scientific theory of plate tectonics. Nor had they heard about the hot spot below the Hawaiian Islands. Nevertheless, the Hawaiian mythological explanation of the creation of Pele and the Hawaiian Islands seems to correspond closely to the ideas of modern science. According to legend, Pele, the Hawaiian goddess of volcanoes, was born of the marriage of earth and sky, possibly in Tahiti. Pele's mother was Haumea, the earth. Her father was Ku-waha-ilo, who represented the destructive forces of nature. Pele emerged from Haumea as molten lava.

There was a sibling rivalry between Pele, who represented fire, and her jealous older sister Namaka o Kahai, who represented water. To escape the friction with her sister, Pele left in search of a more congenial environment. As she traveled far across the ocean, her sister Namaka

A visitor to the crater of the Kilauea volcano left an offering to the Hawaiian goddess Pele.

took control of the seas. When Pele arrived in the part of the Pacific Ocean that would become the site of the Hawaiian Islands, she decided this would be her home.

Pele created her first island, Niihau, by using her magic digging tool called Paoa to open a volcanic crater. Pele's sister Namaka soon sent waves to douse the volcano's fires. So Pele moved on to create Kauai to the southeast. But once again her sister chased her away. Pele then went on to Oahu, where she dug a fire pit near present-day Honolulu. Again Namaka chased Pele away by drowning the fire pit in saltwater. Continuing on to the southeast, Pele went to

Molokai. At each island, Pele dug down into the fiery earth deeper than the time before. And each time her sister Namaka chased her away. On Maui, Pele created the enormous crater known as Haleakala. When Namaka forced Pele from Maui, Pele built the highest volcanoes yet on the island of Hawaii.

Pele's southeastward movement, as she created the chain of volcanoes, corresponds to the north-westward movement of the Pacific Plate over the hot spot that keeps creating new volcanic islands. However improbable, somehow the ancient Hawaiian legends closely mirror the true geologic history that took millions of years to unfold.

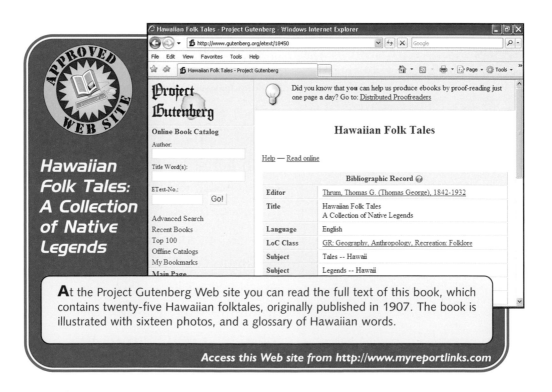

Hawaiian Folk Tales: A Collection of Native Legends

At the Project Gutenberg Web site you can read the full text of this book, which contains twenty-five Hawaiian folktales, originally published in 1907. The book is illustrated with sixteen photos, and a glossary of Hawaiian words.

Access this Web site from http://www.myreportlinks.com

▲ *This statue of Kamehameha the Great stands in front of the Hawaii State Supreme Court building.*

According to Hawaiian tradition, Pele today still dwells on the island of Hawai`i. Her home is in Halemaumau, the pit crater within the caldera of Kilauea. Here, Namaka failed to chase Pele away. There was a fierce battle between the two sisters. Namaka tore Pele to pieces and scattered her bones along the shore. Pieces of lava on the shore are now known as Naiwi o Pele, "Pele's bones." Eventually, when Namaka saw reddish smoke rising from the flaming crater atop Mauna Loa, she realized she could never defeat Pele. She would have to settle for constantly wearing away at Pele's home, sending ocean waves crashing against Pele's lava, eroding and crushing the lava into sand.

During eruptions of lava in Kilauea's caldera, droplets of molten lava cool into globules of volcanic glass. These are known as Pele's tears. And clusters of spun-glass threads that sometimes accompany the droplets are known as Pele's hair. Lava in the form of green, gemlike stones called peridots is also known as Pele's diamonds.

⊜ THE POWER OF PELE

Hawaiians since ancient times have feared and respected the power of Pele. Time after time over the course of many centuries, Hawaiians saw with their own eyes the power of Pele. They saw Pele destroy their homes and land, forests, and even melt rock. The Hawaiians immortalized Pele in song and dance and in legend and tradition.

Down through the years, they have kept alive their religious traditions and beliefs. To this day, Hawaiians seek to appease the goddess with chanted prayers, sacred hula dances, and various offerings or gifts. These offerings most often consist of garlands of flowers, called lei.

In the Puna district of Hawai`i Island, near Kilauea's lava flows, there are stories of a mysterious woman. She is only seen traveling about just before a volcanic eruption. Residents report encountering Pele on narrow rural roads, often at dusk. There are variations in the reports of those who claim to have seen her. Some see a young and attractive woman, while others see an old woman. Those who show her some kindness are apparently spared from the lava flow. Pele's Chant, from the Puna district, warns:

The woman comes forth from the pit
Forth from the river with yellow tide
What ravage!

Welcome

Welcome to the on-line service of the Hawaiian Historical Society. Founded in 1892, the Society is dedicated to preserving historical materials relating to Hawai'i and the Pacific region and to publishing scholarly research on Hawaiian and Pacific history. In addition, the Society presents lectures and other programs, free to the public, on various aspects of Hawaiian history.

The Library of the Hawaiian Historical Society provides a research collection of printed and manuscript material for use

The Hawaiian Historical Society

Formed in 1892, this group seeks to preserve the history of Hawaii and the Pacific region. Of greatest interest is *History Moments*, originally prepared for radio, which covers historic firsts for the islands.

Access this Web site from http://www.myreportlinks.com

Rocky strata up-torn

Deep gullied streams

Toothed are the cliffs

Like an oven glows the face of the rocks[4]

⇒ KING KAMEHAMEHA

In 1790 King Kamehameha, who came to be called Kamehameha the Great, was fighting for control of the island of Hawai`i. His war against Chief Keoua had been raging for eight years. Suddenly one day there was a violent eruption of Kilauea. Eighty of Keoua's warriors were caught and suffocated as they fled the ash fallout. Their footprints were left in the cement-like ash. There they were soaked by rains, baked by the sun, and thus preserved. Hawaiians regarded the tragedy as an omen that Pele was on the side of Kamehameha. King Kamehameha then went on to successfully conquer each of the Hawaiian Islands, one by one. He united them into a kingdom under his rule.

Down through the years, strange phenomena involving volcanic eruptions and lava flows have been attributed to Pele. During the 1880 eruption of Mauna Loa, lava rapidly flowed down the mountain and threatened the town of Hilo. The people asked Princess Ruth, a granddaughter of King Kamehameha, to save the town. The sixty-three-year-old woman weighed four hundred pounds and could not walk very far over the rough ground.

She was carried up the slope to the edge of the advancing lava flow. Princess Ruth offered sacred chants to Pele and made offerings to the goddess. She poured a bottle of brandy onto the grass burning ahead of the lava flow. (She didn't have any of the scarce traditional awa made from ti roots. So she had grabbed a bottle of brandy). Princess Ruth also tossed red handkerchiefs onto the lava flow. Amazingly, by the next morning, Mauna Loa was no longer erupting. The moving lava had stopped at a stone wall at the edge of Hilo.

PELE COMES AGAIN?

On the evening of January 12, 1960, an elderly woman showed up at the lighthouse at Cape Kumukahi on Hawai`i Island. The lighthouse keeper invited her inside and offered her a meal. The very next day, Kilauea erupted. A fountain of fire half a mile long shot up in the middle of a sugarcane field above Kapoho. Nearly one hundred homes and businesses, including a hot-springs resort, disappeared beneath the lava flow. The lava continued to flow toward the sea. Soon the lava flow reached the lighthouse at Cape Kumukahi. The lava flow parted and circled around the lighthouse, sparing it from destruction. Had Pele taken the form of the old woman who had visited the lighthouse the night before?

Captain James Cook's monument marks the spot where Cook first landed in Hawaii in 1778. It is located in Waimea on Hawaii's Big Island.

→ EXPLORERS, TRADERS, MISSIONARIES, AND SETTLERS

Hawaii's first European visitor was Captain James Cook of the British Royal Navy. He stepped ashore at Waimea on the island of Kauai on January 18, 1778. Regarding his discovery of the Hawaiian Islands, Cook wrote in his journal: "An island appeared, bearing northeast-by east. Not long after, more land was seen, which bore north, and was totally detached from the former."[5]

Cook was leading his third voyage of discovery in the Pacific Ocean. The goal of his expedition was to discover the Northwest Passage between the Pacific and Atlantic oceans if such a passage existed. Cook received a warm hospitable welcome from the Hawaiians. He then sailed away and explored the western coast of North America. Cook went as far north as the Bering Strait along the coast of Alaska. After failing to discover the Northwest Passage, Cook sailed back to Hawaii. He intended to return to the Arctic the following summer.

In 1779 Cook sailed around the Hawaiian Islands for eight weeks. He and his crew spent a month on the island of Hawai`i. There they were well received by the native people. Cook had a fondness for the Hawaiians. In his journal he wrote: "We met with less reserve and suspicion in our intercourse with the people of this island than

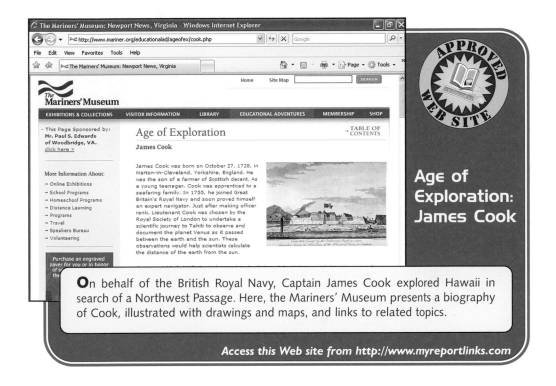

Access this Web site from http://www.myreportlinks.com

we had ever experienced among any tribe of savages. The inhabitants of Tahiti have not that confidence in our integrity. Whence it may be inferred that those of Hawaii are more faithful in their dealings with others than the Tahitians."[6] How ironic, then, was the tragedy that would soon befall Cook in Hawaii.

Cook set sail again for the Arctic, but his ship was badly damaged in a storm. Cook returned to the island of Hawai`i at Kealakekua Bay to make repairs. But this time the Hawaiians were not happy to see Cook and his crew. Perhaps it was because the Europeans had depleted local food supplies on their previous stay. Tensions rose as misunderstandings and quarrels broke out between both groups. Some Hawaiians stole one of Cook's cutters, a small boat for ferrying passengers or cargo ashore. Cook then went ashore with nine armed crewmen. He hoped to persuade King Kalaniopuu to accompany them back to the ship. There the king would be held for ransom in exchange for the cutter. But a fight broke out on the beach. Cook was killed by the angry crowd that had gathered. Among the Hawaiians on the beach was Kamehameha, who would later become king of the Hawaiian Islands.

Within a few years of Cook's arrival, trading ships and whalers were stopping in Hawaii to take on supplies. Hawaii became a key factor in the development of the China

Queen Liliuokalani was ousted from power on ▷ *January 17, 1893. This photo of her was taken around the time of her death in 1917.*

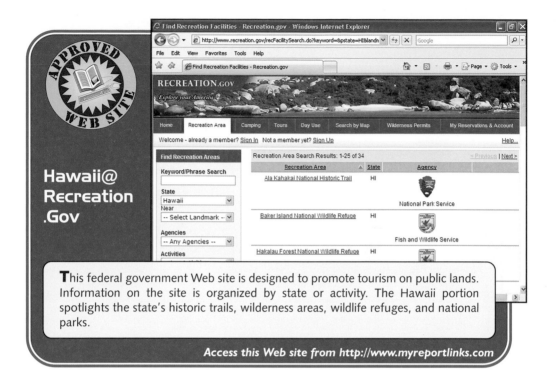

This federal government Web site is designed to promote tourism on public lands. Information on the site is organized by state or activity. The Hawaii portion spotlights the state's historic trails, wilderness areas, wildlife refuges, and national parks.

Access this Web site from http://www.myreportlinks.com

trade route. The traders came from America, Britain, France, and Russia. They picked up furs on the Pacific Northwest coast of America and sandalwood in Hawaii. They traded these goods in China for exotic spices, silk cloth, and furniture.

Hawaii's isolation ended shortly after that, with the arrival of Christian missionaries and white settlers. The first missionaries, from Boston, arrived on April 19, 1820, at Kailua Bay on Hawaii Island. In 1823 English missionary Reverend William Ellis and the Reverend Asa Thurston became the first white men to scale Kilauea. Ellis described the sight they beheld from the edge of Kilauea's caldera: "A spectacle, sublime and even appalling, presented itself before us. We stopped and trembled. Astonishment and awe for some moments rendered us mute, and, like statues, we stood fixed to the spot, with our eyes riveted on the abyss below."[7]

Many missionary families eventually left the church and built sugar plantations on their land. The sugar planters then imported workers from Japan, China, and other countries. Others established cattle ranches. One of America's biggest cattle ranches, the Parker Ranch, was started on the island of Hawai`i in 1847 by John Parker. Today Hawaiian cowboys still ride the range on horseback. They herd fifty thousand heads of cattle on the Parker Ranch's 350 square miles (90.5 square kilometers) of rolling grasslands.

The Hawaiian monarchy ended in 1893. The sugar planters wanted the United States to annex the Hawaiian Islands. They won the support of the U.S. minister in the islands and a contingent of U.S. Marines aboard a visiting warship. On January 17, 1893, they arrested Queen Liliuokalani and took over the royal palace. The Hawaiian Islands became a U.S. territory in 1898 and gained statehood in 1959.

Chapter

3

Volcano House was a hotel built on the caldera of the Kilauea volcano. This photo of Volcano House dates back to 1912.

History of Hawai`i Volcanoes National Park

Long before the island of Hawai`i's volcanoes became part of a national park, interest in the area had been building throughout the 1800s. A hotel called Volcano House was built on the edge of Kilauea's caldera. There visitors could experience a volcano from close-up:

> Volcano House, which had been built on the edge of the caldera when the lava still bubbled and smoked, was the most recent in a series of lodges on the same site. The first had been a grass hut erected in 1846 by a sugar planter, an entrepreneur who charged guests a fairly high-end one dollar a night. In the nineteenth century, Isabella Bird, Theodore Roosevelt, and Mark Twain had visited.[1]

In 1866 a more substantial grass-thatched Volcano House replaced the original grass hut. It consisted of four bedrooms, a parlor, and a dining room. That year, Mark Twain stayed at the hotel and was very impressed. He wrote to a friend that the surprise of finding such a good hotel at such an outlandish spot startled him more than the volcano did. In 1873 Isabella Bird, the famous Victorian English world traveler, spent six months in Hawaii. She climbed the volcanoes and hiked across the lava fields.

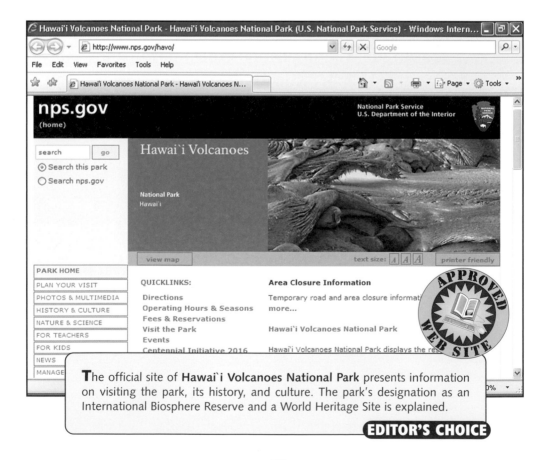

The official site of **Hawai`i Volcanoes National Park** presents information on visiting the park, its history, and culture. The park's designation as an International Biosphere Reserve and a World Heritage Site is explained.

EDITOR'S CHOICE

In 1903 William R. Castle, a Honolulu lawyer and financier, wrote in the Volcano Hotel guest-book: "The time has come when the United States Government might well reserve the whole region from Mokuaweoweo (the summit crater on Mauna Loa) to the sea in Puna."[2] Three years later, Edyth Tozier Weatherred, an Oregon journalist, led a group of women magazine writers on a tour of Kilauea. She became the first person to suggest that the area around the volcano should be a national park. On March 20, 1906, the *Weekly Hilo Tribune* published an editorial supporting Weatherred's idea:

> The suggestion that Kilauea be made a national park meets with a unanimous response in its favor. The idea, after all a most natural one, was published first by the *Tribune*, and was made by the leader of the Oregon party, recent visitors to the volcano. It is eminently proper and in line with national policy that the volcano and its environs should be in the keeping, and under the care of the federal government, for the benefit of the people and in order that its surroundings may be both protected and improved.[3]

CREATING HAWAI`I VOLCANOES NATIONAL PARK

Lorrin A. Thurston did more than any other person to bring about the creation of Hawai`i Volcanoes National Park. He was the grandson of the Reverend Asa Thurston. Lorrin Thurston first saw Kilauea when he was twenty-one years old. He became very interested in the region. In 1891 he formed the company that operated the Volcano House for the next thirteen years. In 1900 Thurston began publishing the *Honolulu Advertiser*. Then, in 1906 Thurston began endorsing the idea of a national park in Hawaii in his newspaper. A delegation of fifty members of Congress and their wives visited Hawaii in 1907. Thurston made every effort to convince them about the idea of a national park. Thurston repeated his efforts the following year with another visiting congressional delegation.

⇒THE BILL IS DRAFTED

In 1911 Thurston won the support of Hawaii Governor Walter R. Frear. The governor sent the draft of a bill to Washington proposing the creation of "Kilauea National Park." But opposition arose from local ranchers because the proposed park would include 1,000 acres (405 hectares) of ranch land. In response to the ranchers, Thurston quoted these endorsements of the park proposal in the April 11, 1911, edition of his *Advertiser*:

> I thoroughly believe in that national park in Hawaii. If I get a chance, I will gladly help out.
> —Theodore Roosevelt.

I am heartily with you in the effort you are
making to have Congress set aside 90 square
miles on the island of Hawaii as a national park,
including the world's greatest active volcanoes.
In this matter, I shall do all in my power.

—John Muir.

If the Kilauea Park bill is introduced in this Congress, you may be sure that it will have my best
attention.

—Henry Cabot Lodge.[4]

On April 26, 1911, both houses of Hawaii's Ter-
ritorial Legislature passed a unanimous resolution
endorsing the park proposal.

In 1912 Thomas Augustus Jaggar began his
study of the island's volcanoes. Jaggar was a
volcanologist from the Massachusetts Institute of

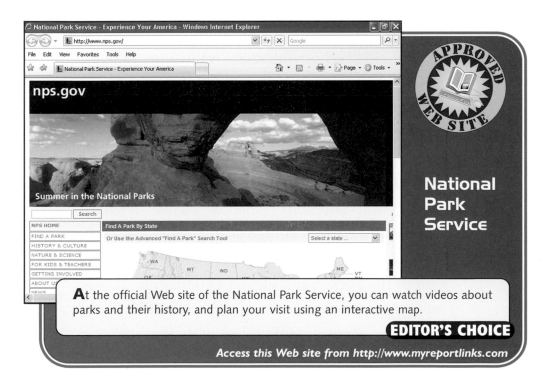

At the official Web site of the National Park Service, you can watch videos about
parks and their history, and plan your visit using an interactive map.

EDITOR'S CHOICE

Access this Web site from http://www.myreportlinks.com

Technology. He first visited Kilauea in 1909 while en route to Japan to observe the active volcanoes Tarumai and Asama. Jaggar was one of the first scientists to understand that contact between lava and groundwater could be very explosive. He had previously studied volcanoes in Martinique, Italy, and the Aleutian Islands. Jaggar carried out some initial studies of Kilauea. He decided that Kilauea offered the best opportunity for the type of research he had in mind. According to Jaggar, "There is no place on the globe so favorable for systematic study of volcanology and the relation-ships of local earthquakes to volcanoes as in Hawaii . . . where the earth's primitive processes are at work making new land."[5]

Jaggar believed that the main purpose of his work should be humanitarian. He wanted to learn how to make accurate predictions of a volcanic eruption and associated earthquakes. This way he could help protect lives and property.

RESEARCHERS WANT A PARK, TOO

Jaggar won Thurston's support on the need to establish a research center at Kilauea. After some initial fund-raising, work began on the construc-tion of the Hawaiian Volcano Observatory. It was located on the north rim of Kilauea's caldera. As Jaggar became more familiar with the area, he became convinced that it should become a

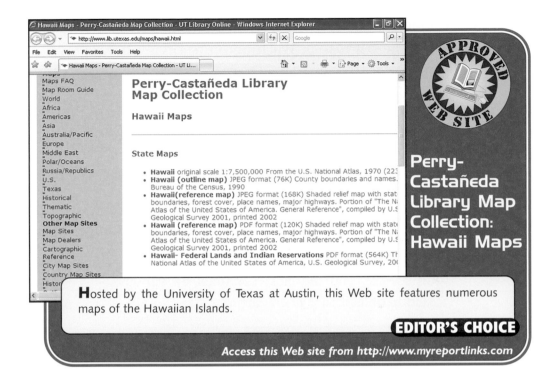

Hawaii Maps - Perry-Castañeda Map Collection - UT Library Online - Windows Internet Explorer

http://www.lib.utexas.edu/maps/hawaii.html

File   Edit   View   Favorites   Tools   Help

Hawaii Maps - Perry-Castañeda Map Collection - UT Li...

Perry-Castañeda Library Map Collection

Hawaii Maps

State Maps

- **Hawaii** original scale 1:7,500,000 From the U.S. National Atlas, 1970 (223
- **Hawaii (outline map)** JPEG format (76K) County boundaries and names. Bureau of the Census, 1990
- **Hawaii(reference map)** JPEG format (168K) Shaded relief map with stat boundaries, forest cover, place names, major highways. Portion of "The N: Atlas of the United States of America. General Reference", compiled by U.S Geological Survey 2001, printed 2002
- **Hawaii (reference map)** PDF format (120K) Shaded relief map with state boundaries, forest cover, place names, major highways. Portion of "The N: Atlas of the United States of America. General Reference", compiled by U.S Geological Survey 2001, printed 2002
- **Hawaii- Federal Lands and Indian Reservations** PDF format (564K) Th National Atlas of the United States of America, U.S. Geological Survey, 200

Perry-Castañeda Library Map Collection: Hawaii Maps

Hosted by the University of Texas at Austin, this Web site features numerous maps of the Hawaiian Islands.

EDITOR'S CHOICE

Access this Web site from http://www.myreportlinks.com

national park. He teamed up with Thurston, who continued his promotional efforts toward the creation of the park. One day in 1913 the two men, accompanied by Thurston's niece Margaret B. Shipman, descended into Kilauea's crater. There they climbed into a lava tube that had been created in prehistoric times. The lava tube was filled with stalagmites and stalactites. Jaggar named the tunnel the "Thurston Lava Tube." This feature has since become a major tourist attraction.

Interest in establishing Kilauea National Park continued to build. In 1915 no fewer than 124 Congressmen visited Hawaii. Thurston and Jaggar expected that the park would indeed be established in the near future. On February 3, 1916, Jaggar was in Washington testifying before a House committee on a bill to create the national park. He said:

> There is the same justification for creating a national park about the three great volcanoes of Hawaii that there was for setting aside the wonders of the Yellowstone, the big trees of California, and the great Canyon of the Yosemite. The Hawaiian volcanoes are truly a national asset, wholly unique of their kind, the most famous in the world of science, and the most continuously, variously, and harmlessly active on earth.[6]

Thomas Augustus Jaggar was an important early volcanologist who established the Hawaiian Volcano Observatory. This Web page, **Hawaiian Volcano Observatory & Jaggar Museum**, displays photographs of the observatory and describes the importance of Jaggar's work.

The third volcano mentioned by Jaggar was the giant Haleakala crater on the island of Maui. Haleakala means "house of the sun" in Hawaiian. Jaggar considered Haleakala to be one of the most magnificent spectacles on earth, especially at sunrise.

The House committee issued a favorable report on the bill on February 7. The report stated: "Strong reasons for creating a national park in this district are that the craters in question are among the most remarkable of natural wonders. Scientifically and popularly, the volcanoes are a national rather than a local asset, and the opinions of travelers appear to be unanimous that this area is of national importance for park preservation."[7]

The House and then the Senate passed the bill. President Woodrow Wilson signed it into law on August 1, 1916. Hawai`i Volcanoes National Park became the fifteenth national park. It included Kilauea and Mauna Loa volcanoes on the island of Hawai`i and Haleakala on Maui. In 1961 Haleakala became a separate national park.

SCIENTIFIC STUDY OF THE BIG ISLAND'S VOLCANOES

The Hawaiian Volcano Observatory has been keeping watch of Kilauea's eruptions since 1912. Thomas Jaggar became the first director of the observatory, and he remained so until 1940.

During those years, Jaggar conducted research. His many experiments contributed to a much better understanding of how volcanoes work. Jaggar measured the temperatures of molten lava in and around Kilauea's caldera. He also drilled holes to measure the depths of lava flows. And he took samples of volcanic gas and analyzed its composition.

Jaggar developed methods of predicting volcanic eruptions. He used seismometers and tiltmeters to detect pre-eruption earthquakes. Seismometers can detect a nearly continuous

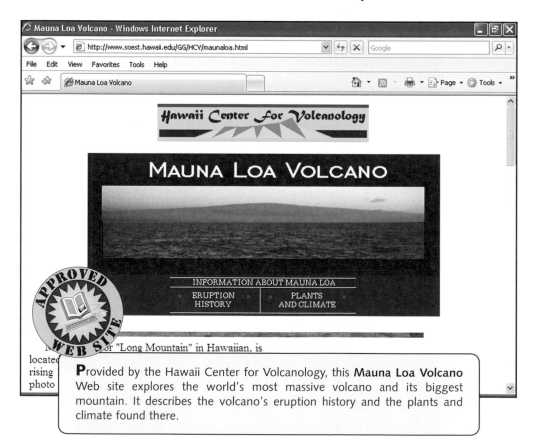

Provided by the Hawaii Center for Volcanology, this **Mauna Loa Volcano** Web site explores the world's most massive volcano and its biggest mountain. It describes the volcano's eruption history and the plants and climate found there.

vibration in the ground called a harmonic tremor. This is caused by magma moving in fractures underground. The harmonic tremor means that an eruption may be occurring soon.

Jaggar used tiltmeters to measure small changes in the slope, or tilt, of the volcano's flanks. The tilt occurs when magma rising inside the volcano causes the outside of the volcano to swell. This swelling possibly points to an imminent eruption. The tiltmeters are placed in remote locations on the volcano. They work something like a carpenter's level, except that they are extremely sensitive. The tiltmeters can measure changes as small as one part in 10 million. In 1982 volcanologists were able to give a three-hour warning before an eruption of Kilauea's caldera.

⇒SAVING THE CITY

Jaggar's research and experimentation also included monitoring the volcanic activity of Mauna Loa. In 1935 a massive lava flow from an eruption of Mauna Loa threatened the city of Hilo. Even before reaching the city itself, the lava flow threatened to wipe out the sources of Hilo's water supply. Jaggar called for an aerial bombardment of the lava in the hopes it would break up the stability of the lava flow, and slow or stop it in its tracks. He appealed to the U.S. Army Air Corps

A view of Kilauea's steaming caldera.

base on Oahu to send aircraft to bomb the lava flow.

The bombardment of the upper reaches of a lava tube feeding the lava flow caused violent releases of gas and lava. This reduced pressure on the lava flow, bringing it to a stop before it reached Hilo or the city's water supply. In 1942 a heavy flow of lava from Mauna Loa again threatened Hilo. The lava came within 12 miles (19 kilometers) of the city. Once again, the city was saved by the strategy of dropping explosives to stop the lava flow.

THE DRIVE-IN VOLCANO

Visitors to Hawai`i Volcanoes National Park can easily get a close-up view of the inside of Kilauea's steaming caldera, which includes Halemaumau, the traditional home of Pele. Indeed, the caldera is so accessible that geologists jokingly refer to it as "the drive-in volcano." The road to the rim of the caldera climbs 4,000 feet (1,219 meters). But it climbs so gradually that it hardly seems to rise at all. As you follow the road, you notice that you are climbing over one lava-formed plateau after another. As the air grows cooler, the palm and eucalyptus trees gradually drop away. They are replaced by the ohia lehua tree with its brilliant red blossoms, the official flower of the island of Hawai`i.

Writer John Calderazzo described the caldera rim after climbing to the top of Kilauea:

> It was a black crater perhaps three miles across with sheer vertical walls maybe a thousand feet high in places, though much lower in others, and it was fringed around most of its top by tropical for-est. . . . From dozens of places on its cracked black floor, flimsy columns of steam called fumaroles slipped out and faded into the air.[8]

Chapter 4

The Hawaiian monk seal is one of the mammals to have reached the Hawaiian Islands on its own.

Hawaii Volcanoes: Flora and Fauna

The Hawaiian Islands began emerging from the ocean more than 70 million years ago. They had a very different appearance from the Hawaiian Islands of today. For millions of years, the islands were barren lumps of bare lava, glossy hardened rock. There were no plants, there were no animals, nor were there any birds. There were not even insects. At first the islands were totally lifeless.

The Hawaiian Islands are about 2,500 miles (4,023 kilometers) from the nearest continental landmass. Because of this, the usual spread of plant and animal life to adjacent areas could not happen in Hawaii. But the lava was rich in chemical nutrients, and there was plentiful sunshine and rain. So the hardened lava was eventually trans-formed into rich soil. And the islands became hospitable to life.

Living organisms found there way to Hawaii by chance. Over time, wind-borne seeds and spores, and seeds floating in on ocean waves, brought plants to the islands. Seabirds eventually reached the Hawaiian Islands, followed by forest birds and insects. Migratory birds, such as the Pacific golden plover, brought "passengers" in the Alaskan mud caked on their feet. Sometimes huge logs from the

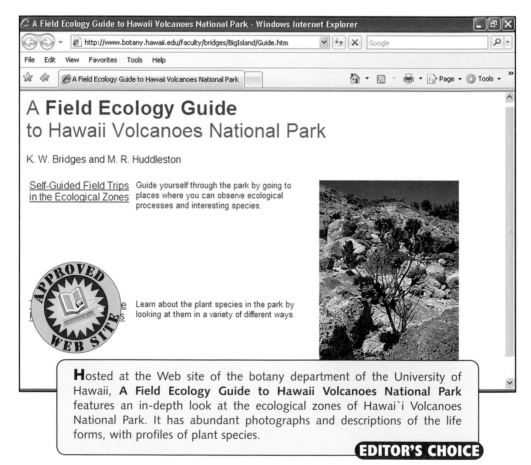

A Field Ecology Guide to Hawaii Volcanoes National Park - Windows Internet Explorer

http://www.botany.hawaii.edu/faculty/bridges/BigIsland/Guide.htm   Google

File   Edit   View   Favorites   Tools   Help

A Field Ecology Guide to Hawaii Volcanoes National Park   Page ▾ Tools ▾

A **Field Ecology Guide**
to Hawaii Volcanoes National Park

K. W. Bridges and M. R. Huddleston

Self-Guided Field Trips   Guide yourself through the park by going to
in the Ecological Zones   places where you can observe ecological
processes and interesting species.

Learn about the plant species in the park by
looking at them in a variety of different ways.

Hosted at the Web site of the botany department of the University of Hawaii, **A Field Ecology Guide to Hawaii Volcanoes National Park** features an in-depth look at the ecological zones of Hawai`i Volcanoes National Park. It has abundant photographs and descriptions of the life forms, with profiles of plant species.

EDITOR'S CHOICE

Pacific Coast of North America would wash ashore. Afterward, the insects living under the bark and in crevices could crawl out and start a new life.[1]

Reptiles and amphibians could not get to Hawaii because the distances were too great. However, at least three mammals reached the Hawaiian Islands on their own. These included the opeapea—the Hawaiian hoary bat, the Hawaiian monk seal, and much later, human beings.

SPECIES ADOPT TO THEIR NEW HOME

Once in Hawaii, the various organisms had to adapt to the islands' unique environment. The islands included an incredible variety of distinct ecological zones. The island of Hawai`i contains everything from dry desert regions to montane wet forests where rain falls nearly constantly. There are also sun-baked beaches and glistening snowfields. Hawaii actually has a greater number of ecological zones than the entire country of Brazil. From tropical to alpine, desert to bog, the island has the highest concentration of life-zone types on earth.

Because of its isolation from the continents, Hawaii became the habitat for thousands of species of endemic, or native, flora and fauna found nowhere else on earth. Given the variety of Hawaii's many ecological zones, the forms of life

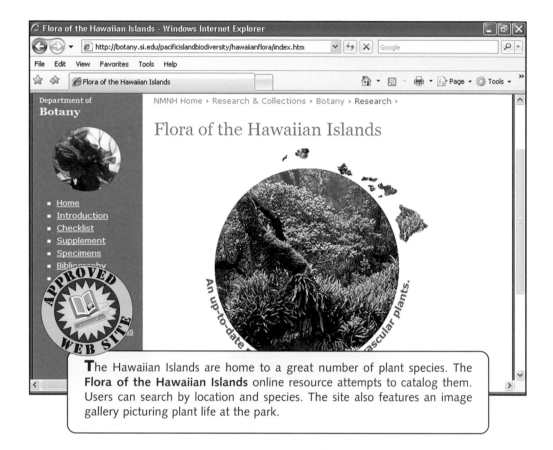

Flora of the Hawaiian Islands - Windows Internet Explorer

http://botany.si.edu/pacificislandbiodiversity/hawaiianflora/index.htm — Google

File   Edit   View   Favorites   Tools   Help

Flora of the Hawaiian Islands — Page ▾ Tools ▾

Department of
Botany

NMNH Home › Research & Collections › Botany › Research ›

Flora of the Hawaiian Islands

- Home
- Introduction
- Checklist
- Supplement
- Specimens
- Bibliography

An up-to-date ... ascular plants.

APPROVED WEB SITE

The Hawaiian Islands are home to a great number of plant species. The **Flora of the Hawaiian Islands** online resource attempts to catalog them. Users can search by location and species. The site also features an image gallery picturing plant life at the park.

that evolved became specialized. Individual species could only live in specific Hawaiian locations. Among them are some of the most endangered species on the planet.

Once a plant or animal species arrived in the Hawaiian Islands, two processes came into play as the species adapted to its new environment. Adaptive radiation occurred when a single species diversified into many different species to fill available niches in the ecosystem. A bird known as the Hawaiian honeycreeper evolved from a lone finch ancestor into forty-five or fifty different species. The other process is known as parallel evolution. It occurred when plants or animals from different species and different parts of the world came to resemble each other because they were occupying the same ecological niche. For example, some Hawaiian honeycreepers actually more closely resemble parrots or woodpeckers than their finch ancestors.

⇒ HAWAI`I VOLCANOES NATIVE FLORA

There are two categories of native plants in the Hawaiian Islands. Hawaii's indigenous plants are those that grow naturally in Hawaii but also grow in other places. Hawaii's endemic plants are those that grow in Hawaii, but nowhere else in the world. The endemic plants have adapted completely to their Hawaiian habitats and have become unique to Hawaii. Endemic plants in Hawaii outnumber indigenous species to a much greater extent than anywhere else on earth. Of the almost one thousand native flowering plant species, 90 to 95 percent occur nowhere else on earth.

Among Hawaii's 1,200 native plants, the most notable can be found in Hawai`i Volcanoes National Park. These include the hapuu tree fern, the ohia lehua tree, the koa tree, the mamane tree, a nettle known as mamake, the pukiawe

The red blossom of ohia lehua tree's flower is the official flower of the island of Hawai`i.

shrub, a native raspberry known as akala, and the ohelo berry.

While hiking along a trail above 3,000 feet (914 meters) on Kilauea, in Hawai`i Volcanoes National Park, you will pass through a forest of ohia lehua trees. Its brilliant red-blossomed flower is the island's official flower. The flower was considered sacred to Pele. It was said that Pele would cause a rainstorm if ohia blossoms were picked without the proper prayers. The sturdy ohia lehua tree itself is a symbol of Ku, the Hawaiian god of war. It can grow as tall as 100 feet (30 meters).

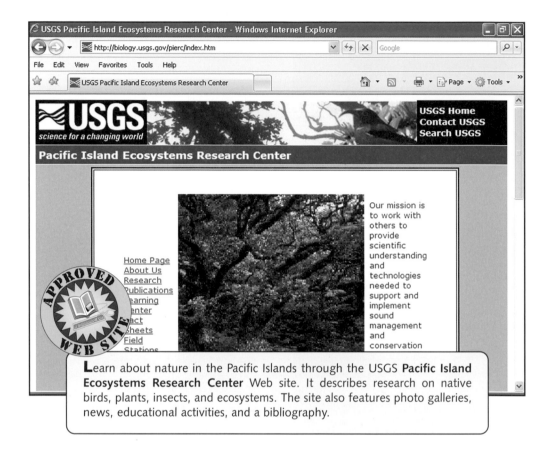

USGS Pacific Island Ecosystems Research Center - Windows Internet Explorer

http://biology.usgs.gov/pierc/index.htm

Google

File   Edit   View   Favorites   Tools   Help

USGS Pacific Island Ecosystems Research Center

Page ▾   Tools ▾

≋USGS
science for a changing world

USGS Home
Contact USGS
Search USGS

Pacific Island Ecosystems Research Center

Home Page
About Us
Research
Publications
Learning
Center
Fact
Sheets
Field
Stations

Our mission is
to work with
others to
provide
scientific
understanding
and
technologies
needed to
support and
implement
sound
management
and
conservation

Learn about nature in the Pacific Islands through the USGS **Pacific Island Ecosystems Research Center** Web site. It describes research on native birds, plants, insects, and ecosystems. The site also features photo galleries, news, educational activities, and a bibliography.

Beneath the dense dark canopy of the ohia lehua trees is a second canopy. It is formed by the huge fronds of the giant native tree fern known as the hapuu. The tree ferns are called "mother of ohia." This is because the ohia trees' seeds frequently lodge and germinate in the ferns' moist trunks.

According to writers Luci Yamamoto and Alan Tarbell, the trunk of the hapuu tree fern is a cradle of plant life:

> The rough, organic surface is a bed for wind-borne
> seeds and spores, and many of the wet forest trees

get their start perched on the sturdy trunk of a hapuu. As the trees grow, they send roots down to the ground along the trunk and eventually find rooting in more permanent substrate, outgrowing their fern mother. And when the shorter-lived fern dies, we are left with a tree of two trunks joined several feet above ground, and can imagine its infancy long ago on a tree fern nurse-log.[2]

FURNITURE AND FOOD

Koa trees can be found in the uplands of Hawai`i Volcanoes National Park. But they are being logged almost to extinction elsewhere because their fine redwood is considered excellent for furniture. Koa trees can grow as tall as 100 feet (30 meters). Their trunks can measure more than 10 feet (3 meters) in circumference. Koa is a form of acacia that is believed to have originated in Africa. It then migrated to Australia before reaching Hawaii. Hawaiians used koa as the main wood for their dugout canoes. Elaborate ceremonies were performed when a log was cut and dragged to a canoe shed. Fallen trees decay very slowly in the Hawaiian rain forests. There are koa logs on Kilauea that are six hundred years old.

At various places in the mixture of native shrubs, vines, and ferns under a canopy of koa and ohia trees, is the *akala*. The akala is a native raspberry. During the summer, there are large maroon berries. Each berry is as large as a small plum.

The silversword is a flowering plant native to Hawaii. A silversword, such as this one, blooms only once in its lifetime. Unfortunately, the silversword is an endangered plant species.

Another red berry, the *ohelo* berry, can be found growing on the surrounding lava flows. The ohelo berry is a favorite food of the nene, the Hawaiian goose, and is said to be sacred to the volcano goddess Pele. Hawaiians would typically toss outward the first ohelo berries they picked as an offering to Pele before eating any berries. Another interesting plant at mid-elevations is a nettle known as *mamake*. It has large, pale papery leaves, which are used for making a particularly invigorating type of tea. Ancient Hawaiians used the mamake to heal various illnesses.

EXOTIC PLANTS

Miles above the misty rain forests of the park's mid-elevation, clinging to an alpine ledge on Mauna Loa, is the endangered Mauna Loa silversword. The silversword is a distant relative of the sunflower. Its shiny leaves have evolved fine silver hairs to reflect the sun's ultraviolet radiation. Each plant can grow for up to fifty years. But it blooms only once in a lifetime, during the summer of its final year. When it blooms, it shoots up a flowering stalk with hundreds of maroon and yellow blossoms.

High up on the slopes of Mauna Loa, between 6,000 feet (1,829 meters) and the tree line at 9,000 feet (2,743 meters) is the *mamane* tree with its yellow flowers. The nectar of the mamane flowers is a favorite food of the native honey-creeper, *iiwi*, which can be seen on Mauna Loa Road. Also in this high region is the *pukiawe* shrub, with its tiny leaves and red, pink, or white berries. The ancient Hawaiians used the pukiawe plant to suspend temporarily the powers of a high chief. This would allow him to interact better with his subjects.

HAWAI`I VOLCANOES NATIVE FAUNA

About 40 percent of the birds officially listed as endangered or threatened by the U.S. Fish and Wildlife Service live in Hawaii. Most of these inhabit the rain forests. About 40 percent of Hawaii's endemic birds no longer exist. Many of those that do live on the island of Hawai`i. And many unusual and interesting birds can be found in or close to Hawai`i Volcanoes National Park.

Rare native-Hawaiian forest birds such as the Hawaii creeper and Hawaii akepa can be found only on Hawai`i Island. A concentration of forest birds such as these can be seen in their native habitat in the Hakalau Forest National Wildlife Refuge on Mauna Kea. This is the first U.S. Fish and Wildlife Service refuge established for forest birds.

Trails through the forests in Hawai`i Volcanoes National Park are also excellent places to see birds. Most forest birds are attracted to ohia trees in full bloom. Among them are native birds such as the bright red *apapane* and the yellowish green *amakihi*. The amakihi is one of the most common endemic birds and is not currently endangered. It is less specialized than most other Hawaiian birds. The amakihi spends much of its time in the high branches of the ohia and koa trees. It feeds on insects, nectar, and fruit. The apapane is the most common native bird on the island of Hawaii. It has a large vocabulary of calls and songs, ranging from beautiful warbles to mechanical buzzes.

The endangered nene, or Hawaiian goose, is Hawaii's state bird. It lives on the slopes of Mauna Loa, Mauna Kea, and Hualalai on Hawaii Island. The nene is believed to be a relative of the Canadian

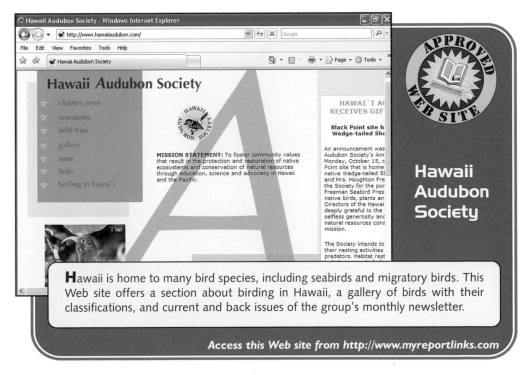

Hawaii is home to many bird species, including seabirds and migratory birds. This Web site offers a section about birding in Hawaii, a gallery of birds with their classifications, and current and back issues of the group's monthly newsletter.

Access this Web site from http://www.myreportlinks.com

The nene is Hawaii's state bird. An endangered species, the nene is often referred to as the Hawaiian goose.

goose, and it looks like a smaller version of it. Just fifty nene were alive in 1946, and the bird came very close to extinction. But today about five hundred nene live on the Big Island. Over a hundred more live on Haleakala on the island of Maui. In Hawai`i Volcanoes National Park, nene can often be seen along Crater Rim Drive. A fed nene is a dead nene. Feeding nene attracts them to pullouts, parking lots, and roadsides where they are hit and killed by cars.

→ THE HAWAIIAN HAWK AND OTHER COMMON ANIMALS

The *io*, or Hawaiian hawk, lives on the slopes of Kilauea and Mauna Loa. It can often be seen flying high above the volcanoes. The io, like so many other native birds of Hawaii, was heading for extinction. But for some yet unknown reason, it made a dramatic comeback. Scientists believe it must have made a successful adaptation to changing conditions in its habitat. Perhaps the io gained resistance to some diseases. It may have learned how to prey on recently introduced rats and mice.

The white-tailed tropical bird feeds at sea, nests in Halemaumau Crater, and may be seen flying over Kilauea Caldera. The Newell's shearwater lives in the forested slopes of the interior of Hawai`i Island. It also spends its days at sea hunting for fish, staying on the island at night.

Hawaii has two indigenous mammals that migrated to the islands eons ago. These are the *opeapea*, or Hawaiian hoary bat, and the *ilio holu i ka uaua*, or Hawaiian monk seal. Both mammals can still be seen in Hawaii. The monk seal lives mainly in the remote Northwest Hawaiian Islands. The hoary bat can be found mainly on the island of Hawai`i. The hoary bat has a heavy coat of brown and grayish fur. Its whitish ears make it appear "hoary." Unlike bats on the United States mainland and other places, the hoary bat leads a solitary existence. It can be seen flying over water and roadways at twilight. The hoary bat roosts in trees, and gives birth to twins in early summer.

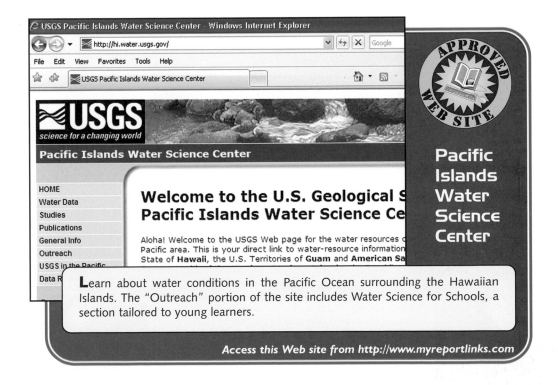

USGS Pacific Islands Water Science Center - Windows Internet Explorer

http://hi.water.usgs.gov/   Google

File   Edit   View   Favorites   Tools   Help

USGS Pacific Islands Water Science Center

USGS
science for a changing world

Pacific Islands Water Science Center

HOME
Water Data
Studies
Publications
General Info
Outreach
USGS in the Pacific
Data R

Welcome to the U.S. Geological S
Pacific Islands Water Science Ce

Aloha! Welcome to the USGS Web page for the water resources o
Pacific area. This is your direct link to water-resource information
State of **Hawaii**, the U.S. Territories of **Guam** and **American Sa**

APPROVED WEB SITE

Pacific Islands Water Science Center

Learn about water conditions in the Pacific Ocean surrounding the Hawaiian Islands. The "Outreach" portion of the site includes Water Science for Schools, a section tailored to young learners.

Access this Web site from http://www.myreportlinks.com

The happy-face spider is an exotic animal that can be found in Hawai`i Volcanoes National Park. It is named for the design on its back that looks like a happy face.

One of the most endangered species in Hawai`i Volcanoes National Park is the *honuea,* or hawksbill turtle. A mature hawksbill turtle can weigh up to two hundred pounds. The shell of this unfortunate turtle is made into women's jewelry and combs. For this reason, it has been hunted almost to extinction in many islands across the Pacific. It is now illegal to bring items made from its shell into the United States. But poaching, or illegal hunting, of the hawksbill turtle continues.

Hawaii also is home to the green sea turtle, another endangered species. This beautiful species has inhabited the earth for over 150 million years. The Hawaiian Islands are one of the sea turtles' major nesting sites. Each year you can find almost six hundred females nesting there.

One of the most unusual creatures to be seen in the rain forests of Hawai`i Volcanoes National Park is the happy-face spider. The small spider is less than .25 inch (.64 centimeter) long and is nocturnal and nonpoisonous. Its bright yellow body with cheerful markings in red and black resembles a happy smiling face.

Chapter

5

The crater of the Kilauea Volcano in Hawai`i Volcanoes National Park.

Environmental Problems: Trouble in Paradise

The most obvious sources of environmental problems in Hawai'i Volcanoes National Park are its two active volcanoes—the reason for the existence of the park in the first place. The frequent lava flows from Mauna Loa's and Kilauea's eruptions have been extremely destructive. The lava has buried any buildings or roads in the path of its flow. The lava flow also caused forest fires that have burned huge areas of forest.

Hawaiians call Pele *ka wahine ai honua*: "the woman who devours the land."[1] But of course, Pele is understood to be a creative as well as a destructive force. The volcanoes frequently wreak havoc on the landscape. But at the same time they are creating new land and enriching existing lands with fertile soils.

→DANGEROUS AIR POLLUTION

Within Kilauea's caldera, volcanic gases, including sulfur dioxide, rise from the floor of the Halemaumau crater on any given day. The gases create a volcanic haze called vog. This "natural" form of air pollution can resemble city smog when the trade winds aren't blowing. Vog has been hanging over the island of Hawai`i since the current eruption began in 1983. Vog consists of water vapor, carbon dioxide, and large amounts of sulfur dioxide. It can be especially hazardous to people with respiratory problems or heart conditions.

At times during eruptions, high concentrations of sulfuric fumes permeate the air in various

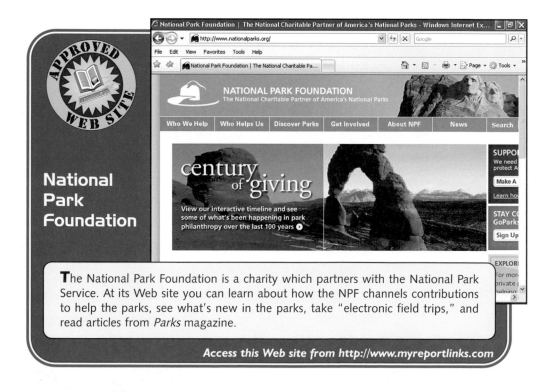

National Park Foundation

The National Park Foundation is a charity which partners with the National Park Service. At its Web site you can learn about how the NPF channels contributions to help the parks, see what's new in the parks, take "electronic field trips," and read articles from *Parks* magazine.

Access this Web site from http://www.myreportlinks.com

places within Hawai`i Volcanoes National Park. The sulfuric fumes can be very dangerous to any person downwind who is unable to escape a sudden, particularly concentrated blast.

Writer-photographer Robert Wenkam was photographing an eruption of Kilauea during the early 1950s. He learned the hard way just how dangerous the volcanic fumes can be. He said

> I felt there was little danger from the lava as long as I could see the opening vents, but as advancing clouds of fume blanketed the area I became concerned . . . a sudden shift of the light wind blew dense clouds of sulfurous smoke directly toward me. I saw the cloud coming but could not avoid it. With the next lungful of air my throat suddenly contracted shut as I sucked in hot sulfur fumes. I couldn't breathe! The sudden realization that volcanoes were deadly frightened me into running as fast as possible away from the vents to escape poisonous gases rapidly enveloping the area. . . . When I again photographed volcanoes, I carefully stayed upwind.[2]

➔ Upsetting the Ecological Balance

The arrival of the first humans in the Hawaiian Islands had a huge impact on the ecosystems that had developed over millions of years. The Polynesians brought with them animals and plants important to their survival and culture. These included pigs, chickens, and small dogs (plus

National Parks Conservation Association

Gettysburg National Military Park, Pennsylvania
© Alan Spears/NPCA

This nonprofit's mission is "Protecting Our National Parks for Future Generations." It does this through education and advocacy programs. Topics covered on its Web site include park issues, wildlife protection, park history, and marine life.

EDITOR'S CHOICE

Access this Web site from http://www.myreportlinks.com

stowaway rats); banana, breadfruit, coconut, sugarcane, taro, sweet potato, yam, ginger, and other food staples. They burned forests, cleared valleys, and terraced hillsides for cultivation. They hunted and ate flightless native birds, and several of these species disappeared. Other birds were killed by the tens of thousands to make feather capes. Some eighty thousand birds each provided their few yellow feathers for just one of the fabled royal cloaks of Kamehameha the Great.[3]

The arrival in Hawaii of Europeans further upset the ecological balance of the islands. White settlers introduced hoofed animals. The introduction of logging, hunting, cattle grazing, commercial agriculture, pest management, and industrial development drove many species of plants and animals to extinction. The introduction of cattle led to the devastation of vast tracts of forestland. In the early 1900s forest managers became desperate to prevent erosion and save the watershed. They planted any kind of tree that would grow, including pines, eucalyptus, and ironwood. Unfortunately, native bird species were threatened when nonnative trees replaced the native trees on which they had depended.

ENDANGERED SPECIES

Hawaii accounts for only .2 percent of the U.S. land area, but 75 percent of the nation's plant and bird extinctions have occurred in the Hawaiian Islands. About 1,800 native plant species once flourished in the Hawaiian chain. With the introduction of humans, feral animals, disease, and some two thousand aggressive alien species, nearly a thousand endemic Hawaiian plants are gravely endangered—if not already extinct. Of the 110 original species of birds considered endemic to the Hawaiian Islands, 40 species were extinct before European contact, another 30 have disappeared since the late eighteenth century. Of the species that remain, 30 are threatened or endangered.[4]

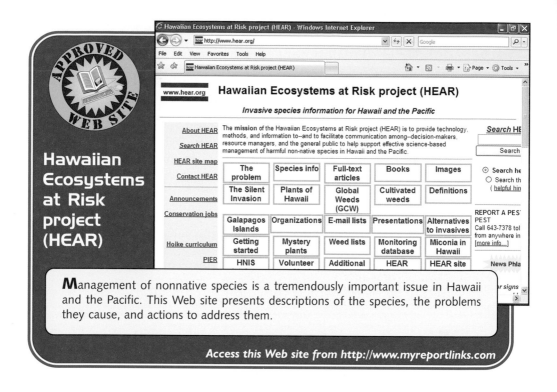

www.hear.org

Hawaiian Ecosystems at Risk project (HEAR)

Invasive species information for Hawaii and the Pacific

About HEAR

Search HEAR

HEAR site map

Contact HEAR

Announcements

Conservation jobs

Hoike curriculum

PIER

The mission of the Hawaiian Ecosystems at Risk project (HEAR) is to provide technology, methods, and information to--and to facilitate communication among--decision-makers, resource managers, and the general public to help support effective science-based management of harmful non-native species in Hawaii and the Pacific.

Search HE

The problem	Species info	Full-text articles	Books	Images
The Silent Invasion	Plants of Hawaii	Global Weeds (GCW)	Cultivated weeds	Definitions
Galapagos Islands	Organizations	E-mail lists	Presentations	Alternatives to invasives
Getting started	Mystery plants	Weed lists	Monitoring database	Miconia in Hawaii
HNIS	Volunteer	Additional	HEAR	HEAR site

○ Search he
○ Search th
(helpful hin

REPORT A PEST
Call 643-7378 tol
from anywhere in
[more info...]

News Pha

Management of nonnative species is a tremendously important issue in Hawaii and the Pacific. This Web site presents descriptions of the species, the problems they cause, and actions to address them.

Access this Web site from http://www.myreportlinks.com

Hawaiian Ecosystems at Risk project (HEAR)

⊕ PROTECTING AND PRESERVING HAWAI I VOLCANOES NATIONAL PARK'S ECOSYSTEMS

There are only a few remote and rugged areas of Hawai`i Volcanoes National Park in which 100 percent of the plants and animals are still native to the area. To help preserve the park's unique ecosystems, the United Nations Educational, Scientific, and Cultural Organization (UNESCO) in 1980 named the park an International Biosphere Reserve. In 1987 the same organization gave the park World Heritage Site status. State and federal agencies and private groups such as the Nature Conservancy are also working to preserve the park. The Nature Conservancy recently arranged for the addition of 117,000 acres (47,348 hectares) of land to Hawai`i Volcanoes National Park. The land, Kahuku Ranch, formerly belonged to the Damon Estate, owned by a prominent island family.

Today the wilds of Hawaii are home to wild cattle, feral pigs, mouflon sheep, and feral donkeys. These browsing mammals are incompatible with native vegetation. Their continued presence contributes to the long-term degradation of native plants and animals. Strict controls attempt to

The The Nature Conservancy: Hawai`i Web page describes the nonprofit group's work in Hawaii. It has sections on the areas they protect, watersheds, invasive species, conservation, climate change, and more.

exclude nonnative animals from Hawai`i Volcanoes National Park, and the park's native forest is recovering.

The park's Division of Resources Management works hard to protect and restore the park's ecosystems. Its efforts are focused on achieving the following goals:

1. Remove alien invasive species with the primary focus on highly disruptive weeds and introduced ungulates such as sheep, goats, and pigs.

2. Restore highly altered park ecosystems to conditions as natural as practical through extensive plantings of seedlings.

3. Restore lost biodiversity in park ecosystems by recovering endangered, threatened, and rare species and reintroducing local species that have been wiped out.

4. Develop a systematic, science-based program of inventory and monitoring to better understand ecosystem populations, communities, threats, stresses, and health.

5. Maintain and expand park partnerships with neighbors for natural and cultural resource protection to target invasive species threatening parklands.

6. Focus on recovery for four endangered species; the nene, Hawaiian petrel, hawksbill turtle, and Mauna Loa silversword as flagship programs for the park with continued monitoring of all rare and threatened plant and animal species.[5]

Conservationists, botanists, and plant ecologists today understand the importance of a holistic approach in their work. Restoration of a complete ecosystem must take precedence over attempting to preserve a particular species of endangered plant or animal. To save an endangered plant requires the continued survival of the insects and birds that may pollinate it. And endangered birds are more likely to return and prosper when native plants have been restored as well.

➡ WHAT YOU CAN DO

Visitors to Hawai`i Volcanoes National Park, and indeed all other parklands in the Hawaiian Islands, must take great care not to damage the

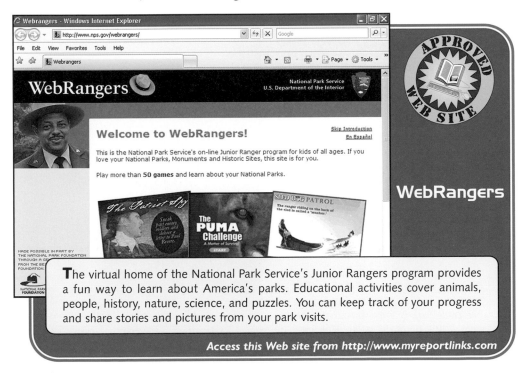

The virtual home of the National Park Service's Junior Rangers program provides a fun way to learn about America's parks. Educational activities cover animals, people, history, nature, science, and puzzles. You can keep track of your progress and share stories and pictures from your park visits.

Access this Web site from http://www.myreportlinks.com

natural environment. When hiking, you should stay on established trails. Straying off a path can begin a process of erosion that can destroy a hillside. Boots and clothing can carry alien seeds into native areas, helping aggressive imports to overrun the endemic species. And picking a flower of a plant that is on the verge of extinction can speed the process.

➔ MANAGING FIRE

In recent decades, fires in the Hawai`i Volcanoes National Park have become far more prevalent, tripling in frequency. The fires have also increased sixty-fold in size on average. There are several reasons for this. The ongoing eruptions of Kilauea have sent molten lava flowing

Perhaps the greatest threat to the ▷ ecology of Hawai`i Volcanoes National Park is fires caused by the lava flows of the Kilauea Volcano. This photo shows what remains after one such fire.

through forests and across grasslands. The lava burned everything in its path and ignited fires in adjacent areas. Adding to the problem are the alien grasses that spread across the park in the 1960s: broomsedge, beardgrass, and molasses grass.

The alien grasses increase fuels and carry fire even farther, exposing the landscape to drying winds. This sets up a destructive grass/fire cycle.

Recent wildfires have converted native woodlands into grassland savannahs. The dry ohia lehua woodlands in the western part of the park are at elevations of between 1,000 feet (305 meters) to 4,000 feet (1,219 meters). These dry woodlands received the most damage from fire.

After several decades of fire ecology research, park resource managers have learned to use native plants to fireproof vulnerable ecosystems. In the dry ohia woodland, instead of replanting burned areas with ohia and pukiawe seedlings, fire-tolerant koa, mamame, and sandalwood were planted.

During Kilauea's lava flows of 2002 and 2003, the lava ignited huge fires. The fires were carried by sword fern and alien grasses through the dense rain forest on the volcano's east rift zone. More than 3,000 acres (1,214 hectares) of forest were burned. Given enough time without another fire, a seed bank and nursery of fire-tolerant plants will restore a plant community. Hopefully, the plants will eventually create a dense canopy to shade out invasive grasses. This should reduce fire frequency and size.

⇒ GLOBAL WARMING

Hawai`i Volcanoes National Park's management has begun to consider the potential impact of global warming on the park's ecosystems. Certain

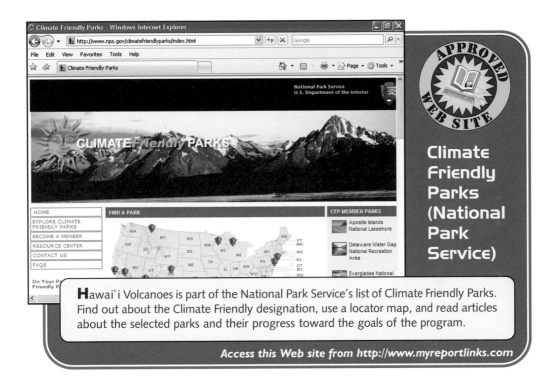

Climate Friendly Parks (National Park Service)

Hawai`i Volcanoes is part of the National Park Service's list of Climate Friendly Parks. Find out about the Climate Friendly designation, use a locator map, and read articles about the selected parks and their progress toward the goals of the program.

Access this Web site from http://www.myreportlinks.com

islands in the Pacific, atolls and low-lying island nations such as the Republic of Kirabati, are already feeling the effect. These islands are slowly drowning as the sea level rises. They will eventually be swallowed by the sea. The island of Hawai`i does not face such immediate threats. Nevertheless current and future changes in the climate are bound to have some effect on the park.

Recently, Hawai`i Volcanoes National Park participated in a Climate Friendly Parks Workshop with the Environmental Protection Agency (EPA). The park has completed the needed steps to become recognized as a Climate Friendly Parks member.

Chapter

6

REC SEARCH   FOCUS   NIGHT MODE

A visible lava flow at the Kilauea Volcano.

Recreational Activities

Hiking is the most popular activity in Hawai`i Volcanoes National Park. There are many hiking trails throughout the park. Some visitors enjoy the challenge of an extremely strenuous hike. Others simply prefer a relaxing stroll in the park. Trails are available for every possible level of physical demand. All trails offer fascinating points of interest and sights ranging from beautiful to spectacular.

Of course, an appropriate degree of caution is often advisable. Some trails venture close to molten lava flows or vents emitting plumes of sulfurous gases. It is always wise to consult park rangers for the latest conditions before setting forth on such trails. Volcanic activity can temporarily close or even wipe out certain trails.

For your own safety, you should follow the rules. Always stay on marked trails and take all park warning signs seriously. It is always a good idea to hike with at least one other person. Do not venture off on your own, as you are almost certain to get lost. Watch your step on wavy or uneven terrain. If you fall on hardened lava, you will definitely suffer cuts and scrapes from the glass-sharp lava rock. Always carry enough water, at least 2 quarts (about 1.89 liters), to prevent becoming dehydrated. And always carry a flashlight in case you are still on the trail after darkness falls. If you plan to hike at the higher elevations of Mauna Loa, or Mauna Kea

Because it is largely unspoiled by human activity, Hawaii is the site of important research on the environment and climate change. NOAA's **Mauna Loa Observatory** Web site describes its facilities, research being performed there, educational programs, and how to tour the site.

just outside the park's boundary, be prepared for winter mountain conditions.

⇒ CLIMATE

The island of Hawai`i's year-round balmy climate is conducive to outdoor activities throughout the year. In most parts of the island, there is less than a 10°F (−12°C) difference in temperatures between winter and summer. Daily temperatures near the coast average a high of about 83°F (28°C) and a low of around 68°F (20°C). In general, winters are cooler and rainier than summers. The climate varies by elevation. The higher you go, the cooler and rainier it gets.

On the windward, or northeastern side of the island, the constant northeast trade winds bring abundant rainfall all year long. But the island's high volcanic mountains, whose summits are almost 14,000 feet (4,267 meters) above sea level, block the trade winds. They make the sunny leeward side of the island the driest area in Hawaii. The city of Hilo on the windward side is the rainiest city in the United States. It receives about 130 inches (330 centimeters) of rain a year. On the leeward side, Kona gets about 28 inches (71 centimeters) of rain a year. South Kohala gets less than 10 inches (25 centimeters) a year. The summits of Mauna Loa and Mauna Kea on Hawai`i Island receive snow each winter. Hawaii's coldest temperature, 1°F (−17°C), was recorded on Mauna Kea. Heavy winter rainstorms in Hilo often bring blizzards to the mountains as low as the 9,000-foot (2,743-meter) level.

⊕ FAVORITE HIKING TRAILS

Among the favorite trails in Hawai`i Volcanoes National Park are the Keauhou Trail, the Kilaueau Iki Trail, the Mauna Iki Trail, the Mauna Loa Trail, and the Napau Trail. The Keahou Trail follows historic lava flows to the sea. This trail can be strenuous, and the weather can be hot. At the 4.8-mile (7.7-kilometer) point, a side trail heads down to the Halape shelter on the coast. Here there is a protected cove that is fine for swimming. Halape is also a nesting site for the endangered hawksbill sea turtle.

The Kilauea Iki Trail may be the most popular hike in the park. The 4-mile (6.4-kilometer)-loop trail descends through an ohia forest. It then cuts across the 1-mile (1.6-kilometer)-wide Kilauea Iki crater. The crater's hard iridescent surface is broken by scattered steam vents. Also breaking through the surface are ohelo berries and ohia trees and ferns. The Mauna Iki Trail crosses a mul-ticolored desert of sun-drenched pahoehoe lava. There a hiker can find solitude in the hot sun. On the Napau Trail, hikers might see giant plumes of steam rising from Kilauea's active Puu Oo vent, and catch a glimpse of molten lava.

At Hawaii: The Islands of Aloha, the official tourism site of the Hawaii Visitors and Convention Bureau, you can explore by island, activity, or interest. Learn history, travel tips, and answers to frequently asked questions, and follow links to Google maps.

It takes a minimum of three days to climb the rugged 19-mile (31-kilometer) Mauna Loa Trail to the summit of Mauna Loa. Only those in excellent physical shape should attempt this very strenuous hike. Along the route, hikers will experience vast volcanic landscapes of multicolored cinder fields. They will see a'a and pahoehoe lava, gaping fissures, and spatter cones. Hikers will be rewarded with views of Mauna Kea to the north and distant views of Haleakala on the island of Maui.

After registering at the park visitor center, hikers can camp in the various cabins, shelters, and campsites in the backcountry. Campgrounds are also available for those visitors who would rather drive than hike. The Kulanaokuaiki and Namakanipaio campgrounds are free to all visitors.

WALKING ABOVE A LAVA TUBE

A lava tube is formed when the outer crust of a river of molten lava starts to harden. Meanwhile, the liquid lava beneath the surface continues to flow on through. After the flow has drained out, the hard shell remains. The Thurston Lava Tube is one of the most popular attractions in Hawai`i Volcanoes National Park. It was named after Lorrin Thurston, the man who was so instrumental in the creation of Hawai`i Volcanoes National Park. Scientists believe the Thurston Lava Tube was created about five hundred years ago. The huge lava tube is almost big enough to run a train through.

It would be interesting to see a lava tube while the molten lava was flowing through it. Of course it would be impossible to be inside a lava tube at such a time. However, you could walk on the surface above a lava tube through which molten lava is flowing. Here and there, the molten lava is visible through openings in the ground called "skylights." Needless to say, you would have to be extremely careful about each step you took. Writer John Calderazzo described just such an experience:

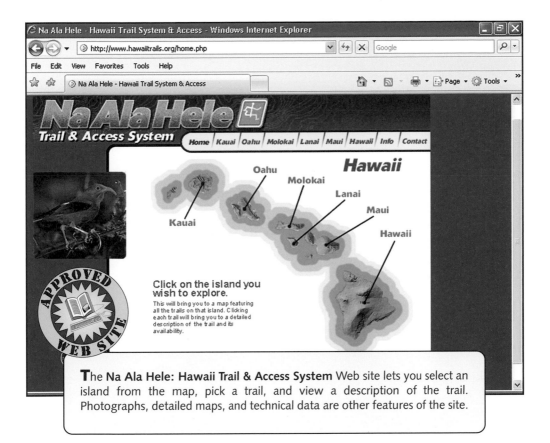

The **Na Ala Hele: Hawaii Trail & Access System** Web site lets you select an island from the map, pick a trail, and view a description of the trail. Photographs, detailed maps, and technical data are other features of the site.

After a while, somebody called out, "Skylight coming." Twenty yards ahead, heat waves shimmered above what looked like a jagged hole in the lava. What I saw was impossible: a rising, red-orange current of glowing lava. That is, liquid, luminous rock. Yes, an impossible river of melted stone surged by just ten or fifteen feet down.[1]

→ MAUNA KEA: STAIRWAY TO THE STARS

Mauna Kea, which means "White Mountain" in Hawaiian, is Hawaii's tallest volcano. It is located

Steam and plume are rising from this lava tube at Hawai`i Volcanoes National Park.

north of Hawai`i Volcanoes National Park. Mauna Kea is categorized as a dormant volcano, having last erupted about 4,500 years ago.

There are thirteen astronomical observatories on the 13,769-foot (4,197-meter) summit. Because of the optimal conditions at this elevation for viewing the heavens, the observatories draw the world's leading astronomers. The skies are among the clearest, driest, and darkest on the planet. The summit is above 40 percent of the earth's atmosphere and 90 percent of its water vapor. The clear, dry, stable air is relatively free of dust and smog.

The Onizuka Center for International Astronomy is located at the 9,200-foot (2,804-kilometer) level. Visitors can participate in a free star-gazing program offered nightly, weather permitting. The Onizuka Center was named for Ellison Onizuka, a Hawai`i Island native. Onizuka was one of the astronauts who died in the 1986 *Challenger* space-shuttle disaster.

➲ FUN IN THE SNOW

Sometimes during the winter months, snow falls on the upper slopes of Mauna Kea. It is possible to go skiing there, an atypical activity in tropical Hawaii. Cross-country or downhill skiing on Mauna Kea can be quite challenging. Some people have a hard time adjusting to the thin air of

Mauna Kea's high altitude. And the snowy slopes can have exposed rocks and sheets of ice. There are no ski lodges, ski lifts, or ski trails. But there are some vertical drops of 5,000 feet (1,524 meters) to provide a thrill for brave skiers. Some people prefer to go snowboarding rather than skiing in the snows of Mauna Kea.

After a morning of skiing or snowboarding, the lover of outdoor activity can trade in his or her snowboard for a surfboard. Just drive down the mountain and head to one of Hawai`i Island's beautiful beaches. Hapuna Beach is a favorite choice. There you can either go swimming, snorkeling, or surfing.

⇒ SURF'S UP

Surfing, of course, was invented by the ancient Hawaiians, who called it *heenalu*, or wave sliding. It became an important part of traditional Hawaiian culture. When Captain James Cook arrived on the island of Hawai`i in 1779, he and his crew were impressed at the skill of Hawaiian surfers. Lieutenant James King wrote in his journal: "The great art is to guide the plank so as always to keep it in the proper direction on the top of the swell, as it alters its directs. If the swell drives him close to the rocks before he is overtaken by its break, he is much prais'd," . . . "they seem to feel a great pleasure in the motion which this exercise gives."[2]

The Mauna Loa Volcano is the most massive mountain in the world.

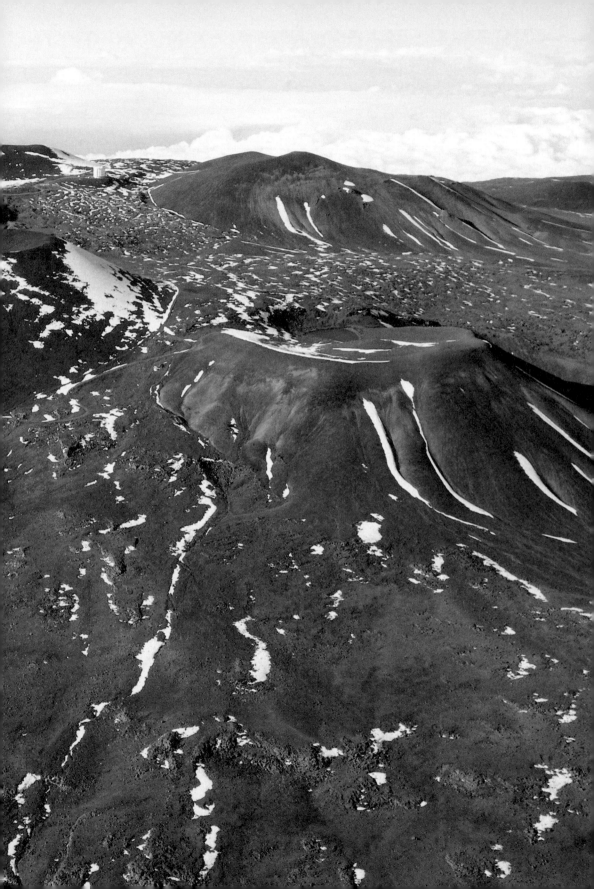

Surf News Network - Windows Internet Explorer

http://www.surfnewsnetwork.com/

File   Edit   View   Favorites   Tools   Help

Surf News Network

Page · Tools ·

Surfer, Dude - The Movie
Matthew McConaughey in His Latest
Comedy: Surfer, Dude. View Trailer!
www.SurferDudeTheMovie.com

Meet Single Surfers
View Photo Profiles. Local Singles into
Surfing. Join Now for Free.
www.Fitness-Singles.com

BEDE'S BLOG...I guess you could call it an opportunity lost. Not
just for me, but for a few of us in the Top 10 who were trying to
chase down Kelly's big lead...

Pipeline 09:54 PM
Archive
B.Door / OTW 09:54 PM
Archive
N. Shore Indicator 09:54 PM
Archive
new Chuns Reef 09:54 PM
Archive
Sunset Beach 09:54 PM
Archive
V-Land 09:34 PM
Archive
Haleiwa 09:54 PM
Archive
Magic Island 09:54 PM
Archive
S. Shore Indicator 09:54 PM

SNN
Click or

WELCOM

HAWA

Surf News Network online offers a tremendous variety of information on surfing in Hawaii. It includes details on conditions, wave models, a swell tracker, tide tables, surf news, photos, videos, and more.

→ THE JAGGAR MUSEUM

The Jaggar Museum on the north rim of Kilauea's caldera occupies the old Hawaiian Volcano Observatory, established by Jaggar in 1912. (The U.S. Geological Survey opened a new lab to replace the Hawaiian Volcano Observatory in 1987.) The museum features exhibits of current eruptions and provides geological explanations of volcanic eruptions. A display of the two different types of lava, a'a and pahoehoe, teaches visitors how to distinguish one from the other. You can also watch a seismometer monitoring tremors in Kilauea in real time.

→ SPECIAL BIG ISLAND EVENTS

The Kilauea Visitor Center Auditorium, on Kilauea's Crater Rim Drive, presents "After Dark in the Park." This is a series of free talks by experts on cultural, historic, and geological subjects. The natural history exhibits include film footage of previous Kilauea eruptions.

Just across the road from the Visitor Center, on the rim of the caldera, is the Volcano Art Center. It occupies the original Volcano House lodge built in 1877. Here you can see exhibits by local painters and photographers. There are also occasional performances of traditional hula dances and an annual Dance and Music Concert in March.

The annual Aloha Festival takes place in September. It features a brilliant royal court procession. This event is staged on the rim of the Halemaumau crater within the Kilauea caldera. The Queen Liliuokalani Music Festival takes place in nearby Hilo.

Each October, the Ironman Triathlon takes place on the island of Hawai`i. At least fifty thousand triathletes compete in qualifying events around the world. The fifteen hundred winning athletes then come to the island to compete in the grueling Ironman Triathlon. The event starts and

**Ironman
Series**

The main event of the annual Ironman triathlon competition takes place on Hawaii's Big Island. The official site provides news and feature articles on Ironman athletes and events worldwide, plus training and nutrition advice.

Access this Web site from http://www.myreportlinks.com

ends on the Kona Coast. The triathletes represent each state in the United States, each Canadian province, and about fifty other countries. The event combines a 2.4-mile (3.9-kilometer) swim, a 112-mile (180-kilometer) bike race, and a 26.2-mile (42.2-kilometer) run. Almost seven thousand volunteers line the entire 140-mile (225-kilometer) course. They offer water to the triathletes to prevent dehydration.

If you happen to be visiting Hawai`i Volcanoes National Park at this time of year, you might enjoy watching the Ironman Triathlon. The spectacle of athletes from all over the world competing in such a challenging endurance test is quite inspiring.

⇒MAGNIFICENT MAGMA

As you can see, there are many reasons to visit Hawai'i Volcanoes National Park and the nearby area. Some visitors come to hike the hardened lava trails in hopes of seeing an eruption. Others come to gaze at the diverse wildlife or surf the nearby beaches. Regardless of the specific reason you may go there, there are many more exciting things to see and do. But whatever you do, try not to upset the goddess Pele!

		STOP					
Back	Forward	Stop	Review	Home	Explore	Favorites	History

Report Links

The Internet sites described below can be accessed at
http://www.myreportlinks.com

▶**Hawai`i Volcanoes National Park**
Editor's Choice The official Web site of Hawai`i Volcanoes National Park.

▶**U.S. Geological Survey: Hawaiian Volcano Observatory**
Editor's Choice The history of Hawaii's important volcanoes, Kilauea and Mauna Loa.

▶**Perry-Castañeda Library Map Collection: Hawaii Maps**
Editor's Choice Study and download maps of Hawaii.

▶**National Parks Conservation Association**
Editor's Choice This nonprofit helps save America's National Parks.

▶**A Field Ecology Guide to Hawai`i Volcanoes National Park**
Editor's Choice A virtual field trip through the ecological zones of Hawai`i Volcanoes National Park.

▶**National Park Service**
Editor's Choice Official Web site of the National Parks Service.

▶**Age of Exploration: James Cook**
Cook was the first westerner to travel to the Hawaiian Islands area.

▶**Aloha! Volcano Gallery**
Get a local perspective on visiting Hawaii from this tourism Web site.

▶**Climate Friendly Parks (National Park Service)**
The Climate Friendly Parks is helping national parks respond to the effects of climate change.

▶**Flora of the Hawaiian Islands**
Learn about the biological classification of plants in the Hawaiian Islands.

▶**Hawaii Audubon Society**
Find out about native and migratory bird species found in Hawaii.

▶**Hawaii: The Islands of Aloha**
Plan a visit to the Hawaiian Islands!

▶**Hawaii@Recreation.Gov**
Explore America's public lands in Hawaii.

▶**Hawaiian Ecosystems at Risk project (HEAR)**
See the effects of invasive plant species in Hawaii and the Pacific.

▶*Hawaiian Folk Tales: A Collection of Native Legends*
An illustrated collection of Hawaiian folktales first published in 1907.

Report Links

The Internet sites described below can be accessed at
http://www.myreportlinks.com

▶**The Hawaiian Historical Society**
The "History Moments" portion of this site highlights Hawaii's historic firsts.

▶**Hawaiian Volcano Observatory & Jaggar Museum**
Study the work of one of Hawaii's earliest volcanologists.

▶**Ironman Series**
Find out how to get ready for a triathlon or just read about the participants.

▶**J. Tuzo Wilson: Discovering Transforms and Hotspots**
Learn how shifting plates and volcanoes shaped Hawaii.

▶**Mauna Loa Observatory**
Vital atmospheric research is underway at this island observatory.

▶**Mauna Loa: USGS Hawaiian Volcano Observatory**
Mauna Loa, which means "Long Mountain," is the world's most massive volcano.

▶**Mauna Loa Volcano**
Those with an interest in studying volcanology will enjoy this Web page on Mauna Loa.

▶**Na Ala Hele: Hawaii Trail & Access System**
View this Web site to help you prepare to hike the trails on Hawaii's islands.

▶**National Park Foundation**
The National Park Foundation helps fund conservation efforts in the parks.

▶**The Nature Conservancy: Hawai`i**
Learn about the Nature Conservancy's efforts to help preserve land in the Hawaiian Islands.

▶**Pacific Island Ecosystems Research Center**
An online resource highlighting the plant and animal wildlife of Hawaii and the Pacific Islands.

▶**Pacific Islands Water Science Center**
Find out more about water and water science research in the Pacific Islands.

▶**Science In Your Backyard: Hawaii**
A online look at geological data on Hawaii.

▶**Surf News Network**
Did you know that Hawaiians invented surfing? Read all about the sport.

▶**WebRangers**
Become a WebRanger by showing what you've learned about the National Parks.

a'a—Rough, broken lava.

amakihi—A small yellow green native Hawaiian bird.

apapane—A bright red native Hawaiian honeycreeper.

caldera—A large, more or less basin-shaped volcanic depression, much larger than a crater; formed by collapse of the summit of a volcano.

core—The central part of the earth's interior, thought to be divided into a solid inner core and a fluid outer core.

crater—A depression, at the summit or along the rifts of a volcano.

crust—The thin, solid, outermost layer or shell of the earth.

endemic—Having originated in and restricted to one particular environment.

honeycreeper—A family of birds endemic to Hawaii, marked by curved bills.

honuea—Hawksbill sea turtle.

hot spot—A place on the earth where rising mantle currents produce magma that can be erupted onto the earth's surface. Hot spots beneath moving plates produce lines of aging volcanoes.

indigenous—Having originated in and occurring in a particular environment but also growing elsewhere.

koa—The largest native Hawaiian forest tree.

lava—Rock erupted from a volcano or volcanic fissure, either in its original molten state or after it has cooled and hardened.

lava flow—An outpouring of lava from a volcanic vent or fissure, either molten or solidified.

lava lake—A pool of molten rock.

lava tube—A longitudinal hollow space beneath the surface of a solidified lava flow, formed when molten lava continues to flow after the surface lava has cooled to form a crust.

leeward—Being in, or facing toward, the direction that the wind is blowing.

magma—Molten rock generated within the earth.

mamane—A native Hawaiian tree with distinctive yellow flowers.

mantle—The part of the earth between the crust and the core, comprising most of the earth's volume.

nene—A rare native Hawaiian goose.

ohelo—Native Hawaiian red berries.

ohia lehua—A native Hawaiian tree with red flowers.

opeapea—Hawaiian hoary bat.

pahoehoe—Smooth, ropy lava.

pali—A cliff.

Pele—The ancient Hawaiian goddess of volcanoes.

plate tectonics—The theory that the earth's surface is made up of several large, slow-moving plates.

seamount—A submarine mountain that rises above the seafloor but does not reach the surface.

shield volcano—A volcano that is shaped like a warrior's shield, such as the volcanoes on the island of Hawai`i.

skylight—A collapse of the roof of a lava tube that permits a view of the river of lava flowing within.

volcano—A vent in the earth's surface through which magma and associated volcanic gases can erupt.

Chapter 1. The World's Most Active Volcano

1. Mark Twain, "Roughing It," Part 8 (LXII to LXXVII), *Project Gutenberg*, 1872, <http://www.gutenberg.org/files/3177/3177-h/p8.htm> (June 4, 2007).

2. Mark Twain, Full Text Newspaper & Magazine Articles, *The Sacramento Daily Union*, June 3, 1866, <http://www.twainquotes.com/18661116u.html> (June 4, 2007).

3. Jelle Zeilinga de Boer and Donald Theodore Sanders, *Volcanoes in Human History: The Far-Reaching Effects of Major Eruptions* (Princeton, N.J.: Princeton University Press, 2002), p. 37.

4. Ibid., p. 38.

Chapter 2. History of the Hawaiian Islands

1. John Calderazzo, *Rising Fire: Volcanoes and Our Inner Lives* (Guilford, Conn.: The Lyons Press, 2004), p. 26.

2. Jelle Zeilinga de Boer and Donald Theodore Sanders, *Volcanoes in Human History: The Far-Reaching Effects of Major Eruptions* (Princeton, N.J.: Princeton University Press, 2002), p. 26.

3. Ibid., p. 27.

4. Luci Yamamoto and Alan Tarbell, *Hawaii: The Big Island* (Oakland, Calif.: Lonely Planet Publications, 2005), p. 186.

5. Nash Castro, *Hawaii Nature Notes*, Vol. V, No. 2, November 1953, <http://www.cr.nps.gov/history/online_books/hawaii-notes/vol5-2b.htm> (August 4, 2008).

6. Ibid.

7. Ibid.

Chapter 3. History of Hawaii Volcanoes National Park

1. John Calderazzo, *Rising Fire: Volcanoes and Our Inner Lives* (Guilford, Conn.: The Lyons Press, 2004), p. 30.

2. Nash Castro, *Hawaii Nature Notes*, Vol. V, No. 2, November 1953, <http://www.cr.nps.gov/history/online_books/hawaii-notes/vol5-2b.htm> (August 4, 2008).

3. Ibid.

4. Ibid.

5. Carl Johnson, *Fire on the Mountain: The Nature of Volcanoes* (San Francisco: Chronicle Books, 1994), p. 41.

6. Castro, *Hawaii Nature Notes*.

7. Ibid.

8. Calderazzo, p. 29.

Chapter 4. Hawaii Volcanoes: Flora and Fauna

1. Luci Yamamoto and Alan Tarbell, *Hawaii: The Big Island* (Oakland, Calif.: Lonely Planet Publications, 2005), p. 42.

2. Ibid., p. 45.

Chapter 5. Environmental Problems: Trouble in Paradise

1. Sara 'Sam' Benson and Jennifer Snarski, *Hiking in Hawaii* (Victoria, Australia: Lonely Planet Publications, 2003), p. 117.

2. Robert Wenkam, *The Edge of Fire* (San Francisco: Sierra Club Books, 1987), p. 114.

3. The Smithsonian Guides to Natural America, *The Pacific: Hawaii and Alaska* (Washington, D.C.: Smithsonian Books, 1995), p. 14.

4. Ibid., p. 15.

5. "Hawai`i Volcanoes National Park," *National Park Service*, May 20, 2008, <http://www.nps.gov/havo/> (August 4, 2008).

Chapter 6. Recreational Activities

1. John Calderazzo, R*ising Fire: Volcanoes and Our Inner Lives* (Guilford, Conn.: The Lyons Press, 2004), p. 32.

2. Luci Yamamoto and Alan Tarbell, *Hawaii: The Big Island* (Oakland, Calif.: Lonely Planet Publications, 2005), p. 56.

Beckman, Wendy Hart. *National Parks in Crisis: Debating the Issues.* Berkeley Heights, N.J.: Enslow Publishers, Inc., 2004.

Gaines, Ann Graham. *Hawaii.* New York: Benchmark Books, 2007.

Goldberg, Jake, and Joyce Hart. *Hawaii.* New York: Marshall Cavendish Benchmark, 2007.

Lindop, Laurie. *Probing Volcanoes.* Brookfield, Conn.: Twenty-First Century Books, 2003.

Neri, P. J. *Hawaii.* New York: Children's Press, 2003.

Nordenstrom, Michael. *Pele and the Rivers of Fire.* Honolulu, Hawaii: Bess Press, 2002.

O'Meara, Donna. *Into the Volcano.* Toronto, Ont.: Kids Can Press, 2005.

Stille, Darlene R. *Plate Techtonics: Earth's Moving Crust.* Minneapolis, Minn.: Compass Point Books, 2007.

Temple, Teri and Bob. *Welcome to Hawai`i Volcanoes National Park.* Chanhassen, Minn.: Child's World, 2007.

Webster, Christine. *Mauna Loa: The Largest Volcano in the United States.* New York: Weigl Publishers, Inc., 2004.